Another Bloody Tour

Frances Edmonds graduated from Cambridge in 1973 with a degree in Modern Languages. She trained as a conference interpreter, and worked at the Commission of European Communities in Brussels for four years before returning to England to marry cricketer Phil Edmonds. She has been profoundly disinterested in cricket ever since.

She now travels world-wide as a freelance conference interpreter, and writes occasionally for the *Daily Express, The Cricketer* and *Today*.

D0620518

FRANCES EDMONDS

Another Bloody Tour

England in the West Indies, 1986

Fontana/Collins

First published in Great Britain
by William Heinemann Ltd 1986
First issued in Fontana Paperbacks 1987
Eighth impression March 1990

Text copyright © Frances Edmonds 1986
Photographs © by All-Sport/Adrian Murrell

Printed and bound in Great Britain by
William Collins Sons & Co. Ltd, Glasgow

For Philippe-Henri, Kieran,
Brendan and Anthony

Contents

Illustrations

Acknowledgements

Adrian ('Go for it!') Murrell, All-Sport, for all the pictures.

Scyld Berry (*The Observer*) for moral support, and offering to carry my bags.

Matthew Engel (*The Guardian*) for keeping me amused.

Professor Gladstone Mills (University of the West Indies, Mona, Kingston) for any correct facts.

The Rousseau family, Jamaica, for inimitable hospitality.

The British High Commissioner and staff in Jamaica, Trinidad and Barbados for so tirelessly looking after our welfare.

The West Indian Board of Control for all their kindness.

The English Test and County Cricket Board for all the laughs.

Tony Brown and the entire England cricket team for tolerating my presence.

Margot Richardson, with thanks and affection for constant moral and material support.

Derek Wyatt, publisher at William Heinemann, who *made* me do it. (Honest, your Honour!)

England Tour Itinerary 1986

January	25	BARBADOS
	31	ST VINCENT
February	1—4	*v.* Windwards
	5	ANTIGUA
	7—10	*v.* Leewards
	11	JAMAICA
	13—16	*v.* Jamaica
	18	First One-day International
	21—26	First Test
	27	TRINIDAD
February/	28—2	*v.* Trinidad
March	4	Second One-day International
	7—12	Second Test
	13	BARBADOS
	14—17	*v.* Barbados
	19	Third One-day International
	21—26	Third Test
	28	TRINIDAD
	30	Fourth One-day International
April	3—8	Fourth Test
	9	ANTIGUA
	11—16	Fifth Test
	18	LONDON

1

The meniscus theory

Some marriages, so they say, are made in Heaven. Ours was conceived, the apposite deity presiding, in The Eros.

The Eros was not, as its name might erroneously imply, some sleazy marital (or indeed pre-marital) aids shop, but an extremely cheap and cheerful Greek restaurant in Petty-Curie — the sort of joint where much stodge was purveyed, and little money changed hands. It was favoured by perennially impecunious, tired and often commensurately emotional Cambridge undergraduates, or anyone who genuinely didn't give a proverbial toss about high-fibre low-cholesterol diets, or the middle-age spectres of arteriosclerosis and myocardial infarcts.

It was in this Hellenic calorie parlour that I was first introduced to Philippe-Henri Edmonds. With true Rabelaisian fervour he was whacking into a gargantuan deep-pan pizza, and a double portion of chips, the lot awash in a slick of olive oil and tomato ketchup. It was difficult to decide whether to feel unbearably queasy or extremely impressed — few sober undergrads were wont to take on a double portion of Eros chips.

He was, in those days, an extraordinarily striking man: 6' 3" tall, tanned, sporting a Blues' blazer and shocks of blond hair. He is still 6' 3" tall, but has subsequently lost the tan and the Blues' blazer. Now he's losing the hair. I often ask him if he'd continue loving me if I were 15 stone and balding. Sister, whoever said life was fair?

More intriguing than his physical presence, however, was the Zambian accent. Having spent my formative years closeted in an Ursuline convent in Chester, I had never had

13

the dubious pleasure of 'colonial' contacts. I must admit that to this day, I retain a vaguely snotty penchant for Wykehamists and Ampleforthians: for chaps who open your car-door first, help you on with your coat, and offer to carry your bags. But in those days, men like that were in plentiful supply. The real buzz was a Zambian who called you 'Honey-Man'; could leap-frog over a row of four-foot-high traffic meters down Trinity Street; and could pick you up physically and carry you home from a party, if generally deemed necessary. It generally was!

Our first dinner date was arranged at The Turk's Head Restaurant, opposite Trinity College. It was a hostelry much frequented by American tourists, visiting parents, and undergraduates who had either amnesed or ignored the last bank statement. The entire episode is indelibly etched on my memory, since Phil paid the bill, finished the wine and we didn't argue. Such a confluence of events *chez les Edmonds* is about as common as Halley's Comet. Since then, we have argued about more or less everything: politics (I don't have any), religion (he doesn't have any); and money (neither of us ever has any).

Life as an undergraduate could be very pleasant. I was reading Modern Languages, and spent most of the time three steps removed from reality in the University Library. The U.L., as it was commonly referred to, had quite a lot going for it. Apart from the fascinating phallic symbolism of its structure, it boasted the best chocolate cake in town, and the cafeteria was always full of would-be miscreants. No one, bar a few wizened dons from the last century and a couple of élitist habitués, could ever locate the right book. Freshers were advised to enter with a ball of string, like Theseus looking for the Minotaur, so that they could trace their way out of this literary maze when they had given up hope. One commodity thus in plentiful supply was other potential skivers: characters who, on the least suggestion, would be happy to make up a punt-party and leave the thesis until some undefined *mañana*. A very social sort of place, the U.L. . . .

After a year of Machiavellian hatchet-jobs on other far more suitable candidates, I politicked my way to President of the Cambridge University Italian Society. My 'kitchen cabinet' ran the Society with tremendous brillo, and very much *all'italiano* — into an unprecedented budgetary deficit. We then did the only honourable Italian thing to do: we resigned.

Phil, meanwhile, seemed to be doing some abstruse external degree from Fenners, the Cambridge University cricket ground. Land Economy was a course virtually unheard of by anyone except rugger Blues, cricket Blues, rowing Blues, and a few despairing tutors. It was not *absolutely* mandatory to be sporty and non-academic to read it, but it certainly helped. In the 1970s there was an apocryphal tale about Emmanuel College. At the entrance interview the Senior Tutor would throw the hopeful candidate a rugby ball. If he caught it he was given a place; if he caught it and drop-kicked it into the waste-paper basket he was awarded an 'exhibition'; and if he caught it and side-stepped the standard-lamp he was made a 'scholar'. Such men read Land Economy.

Phil spent the winters playing rugby as a number eight for Cambridge, having previously played for England Schools, though he got very bored training — they never seemed to use a ball — to persevere for his Blue. His summers were spent playing cricket for the University at Fenners. That was the place to watch cricket: clutches of undergraduates strewn around the ground in the late afternoon searching for any displacement activity rather than study, books half-open in a desultory sort of fashion as a weak excuse for real swotting. But, I have always, and shall always, maintain that the only real way to view a game of cricket is through the meniscus of a large gin and tonic. The scientific principles (something to do with angles of refraction and the movement of balls off pitches), were explained to me once on a balmy, post-Tripos, June evening by a rather dishy physicist from King's. The theory has long-since been confined to oblivion, but I've never forgotten the practice.

My initial ideas on cricket and cricketers were all engendered at Fenners. Cricket was a hobby and played for fun, although in our day (1970—73) the Cambridge team was of truly first-class standard. Six of the players played for counties in the summer vacation, and the captain, Phil's predecessor, Majid Khan, was a future captain of Pakistan. Cricketers there were undergraduates from more or less similar backgrounds, sharing, at least, similar aspirations, expectations, and I.Q.s. How very different the professional game . . . In the summer, Phil would play for Middlesex County Cricket Club. It never occurred to me for a minute that this was anything, or ever would be anything, other than a holiday job. I never watched him at Lord's during that period, since as a Modern Linguist it was incumbent upon me to go off to Spain, France or Italy and imbibe as much Chianti (oops — what a give-away) Culture as possible.

Nineteen seventy-three was a deeply traumatic year. We all graduated, and few knew what to do next. The far-from-academic Land Economists rapidly became millionaires, property magnates, and captains of industry. The rowing Blues, not generally perceived as being Mensa material, emerged in subsequent incarnations as Euro-Bond experts and Fund Managers. And the double-first, *summa cum laude* Classicists and Modern Linguists just sat around filling in job application forms, stunned by the terrible onslaught of reality. Fortunately for me, thanks to one of those completely gratuitous quirks of fate, 1973 was the year when the United Kingdom acceded to the European Economic Community. The Common Market, as many people are now beginning to appreciate, was established primarily as a job-creation scheme for otherwise totally unemployable modern language graduates, which is why, pursuant to the 'Sellar and Yeatman' definition of historical phenomena, it is a 'Good Thing'.

The Commission of the European Communities in Brussels, suffering from a total dearth of English-speaking conference interpreters, was prepared to train modern linguists for six months in simultaneous interpretation. This is the procedure used in multi-lingual and international organizations to facilitate comprehension between different language groups. The interpreter, for example the English interpreter, sits in a sound-proof booth, wearing headphones tuned into the proceedings, and translates any foreign-language-speaking delegate into English simultaneously, or, to be absolutely accurate, about half a sentence behind the original. The interpreter speaks into a microphone which relays the translation to any delegate who wants to listen to an English version of what is being said.

It is stressful work: the interpreter must listen, translate in his or her mind, and speak — all at once. It is impossible to keep this up for more than half an hour at a time, and so interpreters work in teams of at least two, and more often, at the E.E.C., three. There is a great *esprit de corps* among the interpreters in the booth, and nearly all my great friends belong to the profession. They are all very bright and well-informed, speak four, five, sometimes six languages, and are generous and supportive people. I usually find them easier to relate to than some of the 'Madame Lafarge' characters knocking around in professional cricket 'Knitting Circles'.

An acute sense of humour is also an asset for the job. Take the French interpreter in a meeting on artificial insemination who translated 'frozen semen' as 'matelots gelés' (frozen seamen), and a German interpreter whose construction of 'the spirit is willing but the flesh is weak' percolated through as 'the vodka was OK, but the steak was off'. Diplomatic incidents, however, are rarely the interpreter's fault, although Anglo-Hispanic relations were hardly improved at one European summit, when Mrs Thatcher was believed to have 'thrown a Spaniard in the works'. John Lennon would have enjoyed that one.

The training at the Commission was a tough six months,

especially after a rather laid-back three years in the ivory towers of Cambridge. We were being paid to be taught, and no shirking was tolerated. The same criterion is sadly not of universal application in that gilded Eurocracy. I emerged from this *baptême de feu* much chastened, a fully fledged interpreter, and a little Eurocrat to boot. Huge Euro-salaries started accruing. Tax-free sports-cars were purchased. Duty-free booze was readily available. A large flat was organized off the Avenue Louise, the smartest shopping street in Brussels. Designer clothes packed the wardrobe. It was heady, it was affluent, it was fun.

I hated it, pined for London, and wanted to return home. Phil calculated how much I was earning (about five times more than the average county cricketer), told me to stop whingeing and persevere. True love is a many splendoured thing . . .

Nineteen seventy-five, in my book at least, was a disastrous year. Phil was selected to play for England against the Australians at Headingley. He did not bowl particularly well, but with a debutant's luck was rewarded with five wickets for twenty-eight runs. I remember a commentator remarking at the time that Edmonds had often bowled much better, and achieved far worse results. Balls, it occurred to me, are like women: good ones often get smacked about, and bad ones roll men over. Just ask Alexis Carrington.

Since coming down from Cambridge, Phil had divided his time between cricket for Middlesex in the summer, and working for a property company in the winter. His degree in Land Economy and his entrepreneurial inclinations had led him inexorably into real estate. Philippe-Henri, as the name suggests, is half Belgian, and the Belgians, as the adage runs, 'are born with a brick in the stomach' — they love property. Playing for England, however, tipped the precarious balance, and Phil was lost to cricket. What a blow! Professional sportsmen, to my lights, were a species apart: a race developed to entertain the masses, and to pander to the plebeian craving for 'free bread and circuses' — that declining Roman Empire equivalent of *The Giro* and *Match of the Day*. Certainly, suitable consorts in my bailiwick did not include 'slow-left-armers'. Try explaining that to your friends on the continent!

There was no England tour in the winter of 1975. Graeme Pollock, brother of the great Springbok fast bowler, Peter, invited Phil to South Africa to play for Eastern Province. He was accommodated in the Grand Hotel in Port Elizabeth, the capital of Eastern Province, but fairly provincial for all that. It was not entirely consistent with my idea of a hotel, neither was it particularly grand, and someone there was obviously keeping a very sharp eye on Edmonds' incoming mail. I used to sign all my correspondence using one of the honorary titles we had so munificently bestowed on one another in the Cambridge University Italian Society.

My *nom de plume* was a 'la Contessa Francesca Elena Maria di Moriarti'. If it was imperative to impress, as when for example we were trying to extract sponsored booze out of Martini, I might add the odd 'Beata e Magnifica' for good measure. We also created a 'Conte E. Pericoloso Sporgersi' (it's dangerous to lean out of the window), inspired by the injunctions on Italian railways, and a 'Contessa E. Vietato Fumare' (No Smoking), filched from the same source.

We shall never know who was reading my missives, but rumours soon abounded around Port Elizabeth, aided and abetted by the Eastern Province coach, Don Wilson (Yorkshire and England), that royalty was about to grace them with a visit. Don, who was in on the joke, advised the team that although grovelling was no longer absolutely *de rigueur*, a definite inclination of the head and the appellation of 'Ma'am' was certainly expected. Eventually Phil had to step in when Don started contemplating lining the team up to meet my plane at the airport. They were all genuinely disappointed when the truth had to be told, but nevertheless the title stuck in cricketing circles. To this day our vice-manager,

Bob Willis, calls me 'Contessa', though occasionally he does get the first vowel wrong.

One enchanted evening, over some monstrous lobster thermidor (crustaceans in South Africa seem to be sired by the scaly equivalent of Moby Dick), Phil said, in that 'please-breathe-into-this-breathalyser' tone of voice that our Boys in Blue have perfected: 'Better choose yourself an engagement ring while you're here in South Africa.'

I could not help thinking that Mr D'Arcy would have made a rather more elegant job of what I took to be an impassioned proposal of marriage, but there again I don't suppose Mr D'Arcy's line and length were up to much. I did suggest that Phil might come and help me make my choice, but he obviously felt that it was all a bit wet, and pleading fielding practice, nets, circuits, and impending psychosomatic pains in the wallet, told me to sort it out for myself.

An ally in extravagance was patently necessary, and I rang Inez Pollock, Peter's wife. The Pollocks had made us part of the family in Port Elizabeth, and Inez was my big mate.

'Inez,' I said, 'Phil has told me to go and buy an engagement ring.'

'Fine,' said Inez. 'How much has he got in the bank?'

'Four thousand rand,' I said.

'Great,' she said. 'We'll spend the lot. Teach the blighter to do his own shopping!'

We were married eight months later, on the 30th October 1976, and, on going to press, are still together.

2

Line and length

I am, by now, a relatively hardened tourist. Since Phil's
début for England in those distant days of 1975, I have tried
to fit my freelance interpreting around his cricket
excursions. I slipped into Auckland for the second stage of
the 1977—78 Pakistan—New Zealand test series. And I was
there to see my husband's unqualified disastrous tour of
Australia in 1978—79, when he had that much celebrated
contretemps with one Michael Brearley.

The storm broke during the Second Test at Perth. Phil was
twelfth man, perhaps not a job ideally suited to his
Coriolanian temperament. But nevertheless he had fulfilled
his duties of organizing the team's lunch and drinks for the
midday interval. Unfortunately, as the team left the pitch,
some ribald Antipodean made an ultra-personal remark to
Mike: Mike's *amour-propre* was wounded, and, miffed, he
rounded on Edmonds and started shouting at him for not
being sufficiently and ostentatiously subservient in his
twelfth-man function.

Now it may well be that the author of the *ex cathedra*
encyclical, *The Art of Captaincy* is not readily recogniz-
able in this tale. It is imperative to remember, however,
that this was all well before Ian Botham regained the Ashes
and Mike Brearley was apotheosized for it. In those days
he was a mere mortal and subject to the odd tantrum
like the rest of us. Suffice it to say that these two
Cambridge graduates nearly came to blows (note the
civilizing effect of education) and had to be prised apart by
John Lever.

'Pack your cricket kit, and buy some tanning oil,' said

Geoff Boycott to Edmonds. 'You won't be playing any more cricket on this tour.'

'Don't be silly,' said Edmonds. 'Brears knows he's over-reacted,' a fact Brearley subsequently admitted in the book *Phil Edmonds — A Singular Man*, by Simon Barnes. But Edmonds, as usual, was wrong, and Boycott, as ever, was right.

By the time I joined the team, Mike was still not speaking to Phil. Phil admitted that he would be happy to speak to Brears, but only through a medium. It was all a great standing joke among the lads, but it was certainly no joke for me. Touring is bad enough when a cricketer is playing, fully involved and in the thick of it, but it takes a special kind of passive equanimity to sit contentedly on the sidelines for three months, watching others playing and receiving the garlands of success, especially if one feels that omission is arguably due more to personal rather than cricketing motives.

Phil was frustrated and intensely bored. Many tourists in such circumstances, especially the 'good' ones, take to the bottle: highly therapeutic mentally, if somewhat detrimental physically. Phil, unfortunately, hardly drinks, and although still very 'hail-fellow-well-met' with his team-mates, he became introspective, uncommunicative, and generally rather bloody in his dealings with me. I took solace, like so many other shunned, ignored, and isolated wives, in white wine and credit cards. Enough plastic-fantastic, girls, and men become completely peripheral. American Express really does do nicely.

The Brearley—Edmonds mutual non-admiration society persisted long after Australia. Phil's likes and dislikes, however, have never had much bearing on my attitudes to people. I have always found Mike a perfectly amiable, sensitive gentleman, and I gradually began to perceive him as a closet ally. We seemed to share at least one objective: to put Edmonds off playing cricket. I constantly cherish the hope that Phil's exclusions and omissions would precipitate his move into the City, where his agile brain and business acumen would have made him mega-bucks long ago.

Phil, in many ways, is a man out of his era. He would have been far more at home in the days of 'Gentlemen' and 'Players', plying his business interests for a living, and playing cricket, as he did at Cambridge, for the sheer love of the game. Sadly, nowadays, first-class cricket is a full-time professional occupation, and it must be rather tiresome for a man capable of doing other things to have his hopes, expectations, credit-rating, material well-being, and general happiness all predicated on the vicissitudes of an English summer, and the wicket at Lord's taking spin.

Yet Phil perseveres. Every year he threatens Middlesex and promises me that he is giving the game up, but that demon gadfly of talent unfulfilled and opportunities missed has spurred him on to another season. Meanwhile, Mike Brearley, the legend, 'The Greatest England Captain of All Time', has been created by a combination of the hyperbolics of the popular press and the Herculean exploits of Ian Botham. He has become the guru, the fundi, the *éminence très grise* of English cricket. Nowhere, mind you, is it easier to pass muster as an intellectual than on the professional cricket circuit. In the land of C.S.E., he with the G.C.E. rules. And how dumb, mon cher Philippe-Henri, to be on the wrong side of a legend.

Phil bore missing the next five tours with admirable stoicism, the kind of stoicism which having several strings to one's bow permits. The only time he really exploded was when three relatively second-string off-spinners were selected for the 1982—83 tour to Australia, and no left-armer.

'Anybody,' wrote Matthew Engel of *The Guardian*, 'as long as his name is not Edmonds,' and if Matthew writes it, then it must be true. (All right, so what if he is my favourite cricket correspondent? Why else would a dyed-in-the-wool Thatcherite like me be buying *The Grauniad?*)

Towards the end of the 1984 season, a move was afoot to

have Edmonds selected for India. Phil has always been convinced that selectors get all their ideas from the press. Well, why ever not? Where else would they get them from, poor darlings? Indeed, if we could only be sure that they were all reading Engel, English cricket would probably be the healthier for it. At all events, with a Gower wind prevailing, Phil was reinstated for the tour to the subcontinent, and they set off for Delhi in October 1984 to fly straight into the tumultuous aftermath of Mrs Gandhi's assassination.

Five-month overseas tours must surely be a quintessentially male aberration. Vic Marks, in *Marks out of XI*, his brilliantly wry look at that tour of India and Australia, opines that it is not the number of failures in cricket marriages which is astounding, but the number that actually survives. Most cricket wives get a pretty rough deal. The summer is spent dealing with festering sacks of rancid jock-straps and sweaty cricket socks, with consorts racing up and down the motorway, playing away half the season, and never at home at weekends. If, for the winter, the accolade of an overseas tour place is bestowed, a wife's joy at the honour and the glory must inevitably be muted by the thought of four or five months keeping the home fires burning. Women stuck at home with young children, while husbands are gadding about in exotic locations, enjoying superstar treatment and the attentions of accommodating groupies, may well feel an understandable degree of resentment.

Phil and I have always led quite independent lives, in any event, and pursued quite separate careers. I am at home less often than he, and have never felt that short separations are in any way deleterious to a marriage. On the contrary, an independent woman can call more shots and lay down more ground rules than an economically dependent one. Such relationships of equal partners are not, of course, the easy option. The combination of an irresistible force and an immovable object is, so the scientists tell us, intense heat, and the Edmonds household bears the scars of many a

Vesuvian eruption. In the very early stages of marital bliss, throwing plates at Phil used to be my favourite cathartic expression of annoyance. In the end I gave up. He took to throwing them back, and his line and length were exponentially better than mine.

It is difficult to understand the putatively pernicious influence that wives are alleged to wield on tour. Players whose wives join them are generally in bed by 10 o'clock, after a cosy *tête-à-tête* dinner, or the standard room-service club sandwich, rather than tripping the light fantastic till all hours down at the disco, with the unleashed lads.

In India, Phil would return to the hotel at about 4.30 p.m. having bowled 30-odd overs in the sweltering heat, and fling himself on to the bed looking banjaxed. I was all ready to hit the high spots, such as they were at outposts of the Empire such as Nagpur, but he just unloosened his surgical corset and complained of a violent headache. I ask you, is there any other marriage in the world where the man wears the corsets and contracts the headaches?

Wives' trips aren't subsidized, nor even tax-deductible. It is difficult to conceive of any company or organization which would expect such frequent and lengthy absences from its male employees without making some token contribution to a consort's travel. Subsidized trips on the cricket front seem, of necessity, to be limited to the egregious members of the Test and County Cricket Board. A piece by Richard Streeton of *The Times* on the 13th January 1986 included the gem that 'senior officials of the Test and County Cricket Board would be willing to fly to the West Indies to seek personal pledges from heads of government there that England's forthcoming tour can go ahead'. Willing to fly off to the Carribbean in January? The noble selflessness of it all! No doubt a few more personal pledges will be sought in the apposite way by the appropriate senior officials as the tour progresses. Lord's may well be the bastion of all that is establishment and reactionary, but surely even at Lord's they have installed a telephone.

The India tour was a fairly traumatic experience for the team. Mrs Gandhi's assassination and the ensuing riots with Sikhs murdering Hindus, Hindus murdering Sikhs, and everyone grasping the opportunity to have a go at the odd Moslem, meant that the entire series was in jeopardy from the outset. Being virtually 'under seige', and coralled together in the Taj Palace Hotel in Delhi nevertheless generated an excellent team spirit. Worse, however, was yet to come.

The British Deputy High Commissioner in Bombay, Percy Norris, was assassinated the morning after hosting a cocktail party for the team. The murder was officially attributed to some obscure Middle Eastern terrorist outfit, but Phil for one remains convinced that it was a Hindu protest against Sikh militants being allowed to shout their mouths off with impunity in the United Kingdom. A people which lived through Mrs Gandhi's 'emergency measures' might understandably demonstrate a rather nebulous grasp of basic democratic principles, such as freedom of speech. It might well have been difficult for certain Hindus to comprehend that merely because Sikhs were allowed air-time on English television, this did not indicate an official British sanction of what was being said.

There was a degree of concern for the England team's safety, but practice in the vast Wankhede stadium in Bombay went on regardless. Every player would have been a sitting duck for a strategically placed sniper, and these warm-up sessions became known, not entirely jovially, as 'Target Practice'.

These sub-continent crises, however, did not bother me unduly. By now, Phil had made a will and organized some life insurance. I had acquired a modest little number from Yves St Laurent's sale, and waited for my chance to play the stinking rich, if temporarily distraught, cricket widow. The situation, however, calmed down, as these things inexorably do, until they equally inexorably recrudesce at some later date.

I joined the team in early February, at Hyderabad. India is the most fascinating, delightful and often distressing place. Tours to the Antipodes are all very well, but basically Australians and New Zealanders are just the same as us, except, of course, that they operate in fewer polysyllables. India, on the contrary, is a disturbing amalgam of the alien and the familiar. It is a country of violent contrasts: ostentatious wealth juxtaposed with the most horrendous poverty; affluent tourists and even more affluent Indians immured in sumptuous hotels, the one emotionally incapable of dealing with, and the others inured to the mutilated beggars, the maimed children, and the sheer force of Indian numbers.

Cricketers are deified in India. Certainly the team was never subjected to the usual aggravations of travelling in that country. No 'OK' flight reservations which suddenly become 'wait-listed', because a few 'Men from the Ministry' want seats. No interminable waits for baggage at the other end. No infuriating dealings with the relentlessly inefficient Indian bureaucracy at check-in desks.

All these nightmares I experienced when I left the glorious fold, and travelled on my own to Goa for a week. None of these headaches, however, for our pampered heroes. The team had its own bearer, Govind, who collected their luggage from one hotel, and made sure it turned up at the next. Their Goanese travel manager, Charlie, ensured that they boarded every plane at the very last minute, and were whisked away by coach immediately on arrival. The scheduled flight from Nagpur to Delhi was re-routed to put down at Agra, so that the England team could see the Taj Mahal. One player, however, declined the treat. Mike Gatting had seen that old mausoleum before, and besides, 'The House of the Rising Moon' was an excellent Chinese restaurant in Delhi.

It is no wonder that four months of such preferential treatment, and the almost degenerate ease of hotel existence can spoil a man. When Phil returned home and started demanding steak sandwiches at two in the morning, I was obliged to knock him into line pretty smartly. Men, as the ancient

Serbian proverb runs, must be treated like horses. Allow any sort of deviant behaviour to persist and they are ruined for life. Unsellable, too.

A piece of advice, by the way, for ladies travelling in India. Look after your own laundry. Remember that clothes are what an Indian dhobi breaks stones with. Now, this sort of treatment is perfectly acceptable for jock-straps (rancid) and cricket socks (sweaty), but it is hardly appropriate for your brand new collection of Christian Dior lingerie (*écru*), as I learned to my cost in Delhi. To see the fruits of an entire day's shopping in the Avenue Montaigne boiled to the colour of cabbage and the consistency of a combat jacket is enough to make a strong woman cry. On the sartorial front, incidentally, a Sanyo travelling steam iron now seems an essential piece of kit for the tour to the West Indies. The Trinidadian Unions, it would appear, are refusing to carry our bags. Presumably, next, they will be refusing to iron our clothes. Touring, quite frankly, just ain't what it used to be.

The England team in India was a very personable bunch. Many of the old-hand correspondents said (though I noticed that few of them actually wrote), that the degree of team spirit, bonhomie, and general affability was due more to the absence of specific individuals than to the presence of anybody else in particular. (I cannot recollect that Matthew Engel ever mentioned this, however, so it probably was not true.)

Pat 'Percy' Pocock (the off-spinner of Surrey and England), would indubitably rate as one of my favourite tourists. Tedious transfers by bus were often alleviated for me by Percy's cheerful chatting in pidgin Spanish, a dialect he has no doubt acquired around the 19th hole at La Manga club, and which is somewhat restricted to an in-depth vocabulary of beverages alcoholic. My own dear husband would sit totally incommunicado, his Walkman clamped firmly on his head, lost in the sort of catatonic trance rarely seen in cricket circles since Bob Willis retired from the game, listening intently to Beethoven. I felt he was acting like an absolute pseud. His Walkman might well have been playing Beethoven, but his briefcase was full of Tina Turner. I would accuse him of being pretentious. 'Pretentious?' he'd muse quizzically. 'Moi?'

Rooming arrangements for the men on tour are bizarre, to put it mildly. Apart from the captain and the vice-captain, the Test and County Cricket Board has decided in its infinite sagacity, or perhaps its infinite parsimony, that team spirit is best served by players sharing rooms. Not, of course, the same two players sharing together for the entire five months. There are too many professional cricketers sporting single earrings nowadays. No, there is a judicious rotation of roommates so that everyone gets a thoroughly good dose of everyone else's most nauseating habits and infuriating idiosyncrasies. Probably a jolly good dose of anything else going around as well. Thank God for penicillin.

My arrival in Hyderabad was greeted with almost audible sighs of relief from those who had been obliged to share with Phil. The man is an almost total insomniac, and listens to the radio (if possible, Radio Four or the World Service) all through the night. In the early stages of marriage this produced a most disturbing effect. I would wake up at 9 am and already know the news verbatim. I began to believe that I was some twentieth-century Cassandra, and wondered whether this sooth-saying gift could be focused more profitably on the results of the 2.30 pm at Catterick. It was only several years later that I realized I had been assimilating the information subconsciously at 4 am, 5 am, 6 am, 7 am and 8 am.

Originally, I encouraged Phil to wear a radio ear-piece, but the noise still just reverberated around his bony cranium, unhindered by much hirsute muffling. I am constantly being woken up to the sound of the World Service broadcasting in German. It would not be so bad if he understood a single word of German, and yet the awkward blighter resolutely refuses to turn the radio off. It is truly staggering that no one on the team has ever slugged him. And when people wonder why there are no little Edmondses, I lay the blame squarely at the feet of Alistair Cook. I refuse to get intimate to the stentorian tones of *Letter from America*. Just in case certain heavy sleepers in the team can cope with incessant radio, Phil insists on sleeping with the curtains open too. In India the light streams in the bedroom window at about 5 am, inevitably waking any slumbering inmate. A weary Allan Lamb had the temerity to complain, and was immediately fined by the 'Social Committee' for selfishness in wanting the curtains closed. Poor Jonathan Agnew (would that he were here with us in the West Indies) was obliged to cover his side of the bedroom's lighting arrangements with a cocoa-pot cosy, since Edmonds also likes to read until about 3 am.

For the tour to the West Indies, pleading the well-being of his team-mates, Phil requested a single room. This was rejected by the Secretary of the T.C.C.B., Donald Carr, on the grounds that he had received no complaints. Made of stern stuff, these England chaps, not one official whinge. I am nevertheless convinced that quite a few of them will be happy to tolerate my 'pernicious presence' in the West Indies, if only to avoid having to room with the dreaded Edmonds.

I am genuinely pleased to be subsidizing the England team's sleeping requirements, but darling Donald seems somewhat less enthusiastic. He no doubt recalls the incident when Phil was obliged to go to him, cap in hand, and request another contract for an England tour to Australia. I had torn up the original, not, as Phil would have, out of a gratuitous fit of pique, but as a fair, balanced, *quid pro quo* retaliatory measure for Phil having torn up my contract to interpret at the World Economic Summit in Japan. To this day he maintains that he thought it was a gas bill. Nationalized industry, as we know to our cost, is often far from efficient, but even British Gas does not send its bills stamped and postmarked by the Ministry of Foreign Affairs in Tokyo.

As well as this ripping up of correspondence there is another cavalier Edmonds idiosyncrasy which does not exactly square with twentieth-century living. Phil's attitude to bills in particular is perversely Cartesian. 'I did not see it, therefore it does not exist.' From time to time, however, out of sheer cussedness, he does engage in a series of Henry Root *genre* letters, and very occasionally, as with Mr Stenning of *Access*, he meets his match.

A sense of humour is a most endearing quality. Unfortunately, Phil often thinks people are being humorous when they are acting in deadly earnest. As soon as the England squad to the West Indies was announced, Phil phoned Peter Lush, the Public Relations Officer of the T.C.C.B. to advise him that I would be following the entire tour, and asked whether I could be booked on the same flights and accommodated in the same hotels as the team, obviously all at my own expense. Poor Phil, erroneously presuming that in monolithic structures such as Lord's and the Kremlin, information would osmose from department to department, genuinely thought it was a joke when, a full four months later, the Secretary of the T.C.C.B. rang up to give him an intergalactic bollocking.

'Have you read the Tour Notes?' asked Donald. (Tour notes, by the way, are somewhat sibylline pronouncements, applicable almost exclusively to left-arm spinners, and rarely invoked for anyone else.)

'Of course,' lied Phil, who had probably torn them up as a gas bill. 'So what is the problem?'

'I believe your wife is coming out.'

Well, pursuant to the relevant T.C.C.B. strictures, wives, it would appear, are not encouraged on tour for the first six weeks. Something to do with ensuring that the team's entire energies are totally focused on the game. Honestly! The geriatric ingenuity, or quite possibly, the diplomatic amnesia of it all. Have you ever had the misfortune to share a hotel with a bunch of athletes away from home for six weeks? Their entire energies are totally focused on the game all right, but the game is certainly not cricket.

It is admittedly quite true that not all players are unmiti-

Midland Bank plc

Access

Access House
200 Priory Crescent
Southend-on-Sea SS2 6QQ
Telephone Southend (0702) 352244
Extension

2 September 1982

Our reference Your reference
TCS/JW

P.H.Edmonds,Esq.,

London

Dear Mr.Edmonds,

Access Account No. _____

Thank you for your letter and the cheque for £100. Your balance is only £68
overlimit now.

It is reassuring to know that you have omitted to make regular repayments to
your account simply to maximise the Bank's profits but I am sure you will
realise that you have been batting on a sticky wicket for some time now and
it was inevitable that we should draw stumps on your account eventually. In
fact, as you have probably noticed, your Access card has now expired after a
fair number of L.B.W. decisions (letters being written) against you.

Perhaps we were a little hasty and I am prepared to give you another innings but this time it must be according to our rules - after all it is our ballgame. If you are prepared to arrange a monthly standing order to your account here, which will then overcome the major problem, I will arrange to provide you with a new card so that you can carry on advertising our services. A standing order mandate is enclosed which is complete except for the name and address of your branch, the amount to be paid — I would suggest £50 minimum, and your signature and when you have added these perhaps you would return the form to me for onward transmission.

I look forward to hearing from you shortly.

Yours sincerely,

T.C.Stenning,
Assistant Manager,
Cardholder Services.

Registered in England (No. 14259)
Registered Office Poultry London EC2P 2BX

gatedly happy to find bona fide consorts in the camp. On a recent trip to Jamaica, for the cricket Festival week in October 1985, one of the cricketers brought his girlfriend out. It was an expensive trip and the gesture was both endearingly kind, and touchingly generous. It might, on reflection, have been even more kind and touchingly generous had he brought his wife instead, but there again, in the words of the inimitable Tina Turner, 'what's love got to do with it'.

This last of the hot-shot Caribbean lovers then deftly suggested to Phil that I should be decanted out of the team's hotel and up to the Blue Mountains to stay with my brother, so that the surging tides of extra-mural, or rather intra-mural extra-marital passion could ebb and flow unrestricted. Frankly, he need not have bothered. I genuinely do not perceive myself as the Mary Whitehouse of English cricket. Far, far from it, as anyone who has witnessed my performances in the Lord's Bollinger Tent will readily testify. Truly, if blokes want to fornicate their way through the cricket-playing nations of the entire planet, it is of cosmic indifference to me. But please don't interfere with *my* sleeping arrangements.

The auspices for the England tour to the West Indies had not been propitious. The inclusion of four 'Rebels', players who had had sporting links with South Africa, had ruffled quite a few anti-apartheid feathers. Trouble was brewing with the unions in Trinidad. In particular, there was a threat to make the team's stay as uncomfortable as possible, and to boycott English cricket correspondents' copy.

The England 'B' team's tour to Bangladesh and Zimbabwe had already been unilaterally cancelled at the last minute. Phil and I heard the captain, Mark Nicholas, being interviewed on the radio, and refusing wisely to draw any analogy between that sorry state of affairs, and the forthcoming 'A' team trip to the West Indies. He came across as very well informed, diplomatic and articulate — true captain material. The T.C.C.B. should seriously consider nominating such individuals as the 'Official Player-Spokesman', and banning those somewhat less incandescently brilliant characters who specialize in exacerbating already tinder-like situations and creating diplomatic incidents, from opening their mouths. Such chaps should be encouraged simply to repeat, 'I only wanted to play cricket, Brian.' Nothing too difficult there. No word of more than two syllables. Most of them should be able to learn it, in time, and it would keep an awful lot of people out of hot water.

The news of the sudden cancellations was, nevertheless, another nail in the coffin of international sport. Right up until the day of departure, the press and media were speculating on whether the Rebels' presence in the England team would jeopardize the tour to the West Indies. 'Could be serious,' said Phil, listening to a Radio Four assessment. He had no idea quite how serious. I had already spent an advance I had not received, for a book I had not written, on a tour that might not take place, in the Calypso Room at Harrod's.

3

The cricket widow

I dropped Phil off at an ungodly hour on the morning of the 25th January 1986 so that he could join in the pre-departure champagne breakfast at the Excelsior Hotel, Heathrow. I was kindly invited to join the proceedings but since, typically, under a full-length, black-Glamma mink I was sporting a pair of bright red 'Manchester United Forever' pyjamas, I was obliged graciously to decline.

I returned home to a sad and empty house, a real estate replica of the Marie-Céleste: half-eaten pieces of toast and a lukewarm pot of tea, the bedroom strewn with the emptied boxes of sponsored 'gimmies'. (A 'gimmie', for etymologists, is anything cricketers receive either free or sponsored. In Phil's case they range from cars, Johnnie Walker whisky, Hine cognac, Gray Nicholls cricket gear, Austin Reed clothes and Duncan Fearnley sportswear.)

I felt an acute sense of loss and pain and yet, simultaneously, a very real sense of relief, probably the same sort of feeling people experience when their thrombosed haemorrhoids are removed. I immediately contracted a psychosomatic bout of 'flu, and took to my bed for the day with an armful of scurrilous Spanish magazines: 'all you never wanted to know about Julio Iglesias' sex life — 20 times a night, and crooning in between'. Why on earth am I not reading *Unamuno?*

I woke that night with a start at about midnight, the burglar alarm bleeping loudly and ringing shrilly. Someone in the garden had been trying to force the french-windows, the inevitable consequence of everyone in the area knowing Phil, where he lives, and the fact that the England team left today. Distressed and shivering, I turned on all the lights and the radio, fetched a cricket bat from the gyp-room, and in a final, pathetic effort to con any intruder, constructed a sleeping partner from a spare duvet and a cricket helmet. I have been sleeping with him now for three nights, and have genuinely grown attached to him. At least he does not listen to the radio.

Only one week of this cricket widowhood, thank goodness. I leave for Jamaica on the 1st February, to join my brother who is an eye-surgeon, a 'little-bannister-on-the-stairway-of-life' in Kingston. More of him later. The team arrives there on the 11th, but I shall not be staying with my husband until we move on to Trinidad on the 27th. That encompasses the first six weeks of the tour, and the Word of the T.C.C.B. Touring Notes will be complied with, as it always shall be, now and forever, world without end, Amen.

I had been saying goodbye to Phil for the best part of two weeks and even accompanied him on his mandatory check-up at the Edgbaston Health Clinic. The pre-tour fitness test is always a difficult hurdle to negotiate so soon after Christmas. Phil was concerned about his weight, as well he might be, after a fairly sybaritic festive season. His efforts to diet revolved around foie gras with truffles, canard à l'orange, slabs of Stilton, Godiva chocolates, and then a quick post-prandial sweat-session reading *The Financial Times* in the Turkish baths at the R.A.C. Club, Pall Mall.

We drove up to Edgbaston, and stopped at The Plough and Harrow, for a pre-weigh-in sauna. I suggested mega-doses of diuretics, or, failing that, the easy way of losing 20 pounds of ugly fat: chopping his head off. Phil, whose common sense I often have my doubts about, was seriously wondering whether standing on one leg would make any difference to the scales.

All these shenanigans, however, were totally in vain, as nothing escapes Bernard Thomas' remoreless eye. Bernard has been the England team's physiotherapist at home and on tour for the past 16 years, though sadly he has been obliged to retire from touring this year, because of family and professional commitments. He has become the father-figure, mentor, and shoulder to cry on for many a homesick tourist, and he and his wife Joan will be sadly missed in the West Indies.

Phil was told to lose four kilos, having weighed in at exactly 100. I hit the scales at 50, so now we all know what is meant by the better half, and precisely why two can live as cheaply as one. Most of the team, it appeared, were just slightly overweight, with one rather dramatic exception who was told to lose 13 kilos. It would be unkind indeed to mention any names, but suffice it to say that it was he who would opt for the Chinese restaurant rather than the Taj Mahal.

Phil's absence at least gave me the excuse and/or chance to put in some homework on this here book. My publisher, Derek Wyatt, suggested I read C.L.R. James' *Beyond A Boundary*. I did. It was not exactly your average run-of-the-mill cricket book. And it raised quite a few questions about the nature and role of cricket and politics in the Caribbean. Undaunted, I set off with Derek to meet C.L.R. himself.

'What the Hell d'you want to go there for?' asked our Cockney cab driver, more at home with a Park Lane fare than down-town Brixton. 'Twenty-three muggings in the past week. Not safe for white people.'

'We'll take our chance,' said Derek, undeterred.

We walked the last few streets through a thriving, noisy, street market, the stalls piled high with esoteric, tropical produce: huge, dark avocados, monstrous green paw-paws, large ugly bread-fruit, and strange, round, yellowish vegetables, flesh bursting to expose large, black, grape-sized pods — ackee. I stuck close to Derek, feeling like a Burberried stranger in a rainy-day fruit and vegetable paradise, the ubiquitous Yuppy uniform of Knightsbridge standing out like a sore, white, shower-proof thumb in Brixton.

The numberless door was opened by a huge, burly, and not-entirely-delighted-to-see-us West Indian.

'Who are you?' he enquired brusquely.

'Derek Wyatt, publisher, William Heinemann,' replied Derek, 'And Frances Edmonds, wife of self-confessed England all-rounder, Phil. We've come to see C.L.R.'

The surly expression broke into a beaming smile: sunshine after clouds. 'Come in,' he said. 'You're very welcome. I'm C.L.R.'s nephew.' We all started to smile, and shook hands. A great weight of unspoken suspicion, it appeared, had been lifted. How fortunate, intoned Derek, *sotto voce ma molto paedagogico*, that I had neglected to wear my favourite Krugerrand bracelet.

The nephew, we learned as he directed us to his uncle's room, had made a television documentary for Channel Four on Viv Richards, the West Indian captain, a programme we had both seen and enjoyed over the Christmas period.

C.L.R. James was sitting in his chair, a thin, frail old man in his eighties. His pure white hair contrasted sharply with his dark brown skin, and his entire face was lit by the penetrating bright blue eyes. His long, elegant fingers moved rhythmically to the soft cadences of his speech, and his hands shook alarmingly as he drank warm milk and honey. Prisoner of this feeble frame, he might be, but his mind and intellect still penetrated Sabatier-sharp: a brand-new Porsche engine in a 60s Cinquecento. The ideas and anecdotes flowed in a seamless continuum of conversation, only occasionally punctuated by the odd far-away look, pregnant with memories of things we could not possibly begin to know or comprehend. The room was lined with bookshelves heaving with weighty tomes on art, music, history, Marx, politics and literature as well as cricket. A video of Mozart's *Don Giovanni*, balanced with precarious incongruity on a copy of the 1984 *Wisden*. This was the room of a Renaissance man.

In a spidery hand, he autographed my copy of *Beyond a Boundary*, a semi-autobiographical account of his childhood in Trinidad, and experiences as a journalist in England. It embraces cricket, cricketing personalities, philosophy, sociology, culture, politics and art. It constitutes compulsory reading for any visitor to the English-speaking Caribbean, and a seminal work for cricket aficionados everywhere.

'The tour will go ahead,' said C.L.R. 'Oh, some of the anti-apartheid activist lobbies will make a lot of noise, they'll make their political point. But they love their cricket too much in the West Indies to let it be disrupted.'

At the moment, much of this activist energy is being perversely focused around Bernard Julien. B.J., a brilliant all-rounder, is now a pariah in his native Trinidad, banned from cricket for life for joining the 'rebel' West Indians who went to South Africa in 1983. It seems quite grossly unfair to the Anti-Apartheid movement that the relatively affluent, professional England cricketers should have been banned for a mere three years for an action which involved a life ban for more impecunious, struggling West Indian amateurs. The choice of Gooch, Emburey, Willey and Taylor to tour the West Indies so soon after the expiry of their sentence is therefore causing much dissension in West Indian political circles, despite an International Cricket Council ruling that no country must attempt to interfere with the selection policy of any other.

'How is it,' asked Derek, 'that even Clive Lloyd, a man so universally loved, admired, and respected, a captain capable of galvanizing a unified and unbeatable team after years of inter-island bickering and jealousy . . . How is it that even he could not stop the West Indian rebels from going to South Africa?'

C.L.R. shook his snowy head in slow and silent sorrow. Every man, he appeared to be saying, every man has his price.

It is difficult, objectively, to be hard on the West Indian rebels. West Indian cricketers are not paid at club level, and as amateurs they are therefore obliged to seek work in order to make a living. In developing countries, where 30 per cent unemployment is the norm, this is easier said than done. The players who went to South Africa, unlike our own, were on the fringes of the Test side, and therefore struggling financially, since the monetary chasm between Test-players and 'also-rans' is enormous.

For people, however, who have struggled long and hard to cast off the white, imperial yoke, who have fought and died to achieve emancipation, independence and racial pride, 'sorties' to South Africa to make a few bucks can never 'officially' be forgiven. The cankerous tendrils of apartheid are deemed to contaminate any sportsman who has played there. Who should say whether this is right or wrong? In the West Indies it is simply inevitable. It remains a part of the world where it is dangerously ingenuous to think of cricket as a mere game. Caribbean cricket forms an integral, probably even a predominant, part of a complex social, political, and philosophical nexus, a web from which it is totally indivisible.

'Cricket is the only unifying factor in the West Indies,' said C.L.R.

'The West Indies have absolutely no sense of history. *No sense*. The only thing they have in common is cricket. And that is precisely why the tour will go ahead. Cricket is the only thing that binds them all together.'

We left C.L.R. to his books, his thoughts and his Caribbean memories, and emerged once again to the icy flurries of Brixton rain. The next three months will tell whether the Grand Old Man of West Indian Letters still has his finger on the political pulse.

4

Jamaica, at last

I was decanted from the plane after twelve hours and three bottles of Veuve Clicquot, imbued with vague feelings of relaxed bonhomie and fizzy flatulence. Heathrow airport was already a best forgotten hazard, a perilous obstacle course between the Scylla of machine gun toting policemen, and the Charybdis of overladen West Indians manipulating maverick airport trolleys.

Packing had been relatively easy once I'd decided to borrow one of Phil's 'coffins'. I'd had to make some small changes to the name painted on the bag. I'd added 'MRS' and 'NOT' to 'PHIL EDMONDS' and 'THE ENGLAND TOURING TEAM' markings. The Trinidadian unions had already warned that they would not handle the team's baggage. I hoped these adjuncts would prove a useful distinction and determine which of us had the greater sense of humour. Besides, I'd never had a sporting link with South Africa in my life.

A stocky Customs lady, a recent graduate from the 'John McEnroe School of Charm', decided to dissect the contents of my baggage item by item. Her eye alighted suspiciously on some high-potency Supradyn vitamin pills. These little brown torpedoes purport to be the universal panacea for everything from split nails to pre- post- and interim-menstrual tension, and I suffer from a constant combination of all four. It took some time to convince her that only traders of the Coals to Newcastle variety would be carrying drugs to Jamaica, and swallowed half a dozen to prove it. My Braun Lady-Shave also occasioned childlike fascination and another 20 minute grilling. But for possible allegations of attempted bribery and corruption, I was sorely tempted to give her the wretched thing. Her need seemed so much greater than mine, as a surreptitious, anthropological glance at her legs revealed.

'You an England Cricketer wife?' she asked, when all my most intimate possessions had been well and truly raped and pillaged.

I nodded in the affirmative.

'Our boys gonna murder you,' she gloated, her sour face expressionless.

I felt a sudden totally atypical surge of maternal protectiveness. The siege, it seemed, was on.

My brother, Brendan, was waiting patiently as I was eventually disgorged into the oppressively sticky Jamaican night. Brendan is an eye surgeon in Kingston, and researching into Sickle Cell Anaemia. Who could have known what the Fates held in store? Shortly he was to emerge as the England Touring Team's honorary ophthalmologist.

Brendan is one of those uncompromising young men suffering from a bad dose of conscience and principles. He is probably a terminal case of True Socialism. At Cambridge he read both Medical Sciences and Social and Political Sciences, an explosive combination which strikes fear and trembling into the conservative hearts of English medical circles. Even a wishy-washy socialist of the David Owen mould is, they feel, already one medico-political viper too many to have been nurtured in the British Medical Association bosom. He has that haunted, ascetic look about him, and that messianic glint to the eye common in Men With a Mission. It is a constant source of amazement to me that such a genetic mutant crept its way into a family of which I am a member. But in Jamaica, he reckons, there is work to be done.

Cricket, and its significance in the West Indies, must always be viewed as the golden thread running through an otherwise often dowdy Caribbean tapestry of poverty, unemployment, disaffection and general economic depression. A visit to the Medical Research Council Sickle Cell Unit on the campus of the University of the West Indies made that abundantly clear. Sickle Cell is a trait which is present in seven per cent of all West Indians, and leads to actual disease in fifteen per cent of all those affected. In simple terms, Sickle Cell disease is an hereditary abnormality of the blood, causing an occlusion of blood vessels, which manifests itself in leg ulcers, bone pains, kidney failure, and in children, a pre-disposition to pneumonia — often fatal. In the eye, Sickle Cell may cause lesions leading to retinal detachment, and eventual blindness.

It is a disease which does not affect white people, and has thus far been the subject of little research. Awareness of the problem is, however, growing. Clive Lloyd's wife, Waveney, a fully-trained psychiatric nurse (every cricketer should have one), told me during my last visit to Jamaica for the Cricket 'Festival Week', that Clive donates half of every charity cheque he receives to research in this relatively uncharted area. A man of his people, Clive Lloyd.

In Brendan's full waiting room, I met sixteen-year-old Everton. He was blind in his left eye and there was a chance my brother could save his remaining sight by lasering the potentially blinding lesions at the back of his right eye.

Everton had been travelling since 4.30 am in order to reach the unit from Montego Bay, and he was still impeccably dressed in a white, Sunday-best shirt, the crease in his trousers razor-sharp. He was understandably tired, probably frightened and certainly in no mood for trivial, female conversation, until I produced a copy of *The Cricketer* magazine. A superb head and shoulders portrait of Viv Richards fronted the issue, with a rather less ostentatious photo of, and piece by, my own dear husband in the middle. The physiognomy of Everton's whole face changed immediately, as he broke into a flashing, white smile. Everton was, of course, a fast bowler. 'Quick, man, I mean *real* quick.'

He proceeded to give me the low-down on the entire Jamaican team.

'Patrick Patterson. Make no difference if you blind or not, man, no one sees Patrick.'

And he also propounded his views on possible West Indian selection policy.

'Sabina Park is one fast wicket, man, I mean real fast.'

'No hope for the spinners, then?' I enquired, not a little interessée.

'No, man. They roll that wicket for Mikey and the boys.'

'Strange,' I mused. 'When we were here for Jamaica Festival Week, my husband got Viv twice.'

'Man, you never told me you was married to Phil Edmonds!'

Such an encyclopaedic knowledge of the game — in a country where only a few of the very affluent can afford television 'dishes', and where the coverage of the cricket is virtually restricted to newspapers and radio — is truly remarkable. Top cricketers are known fondly and fraternally by their forenames: Viv, Clive, Mikey, and Gordon: an accolade of fame, intimacy and affection accorded to few English cricketers.

Everton sat devouring *The Cricketer* voraciously with his one good eye. For want of anything more substantial in the way of cricketabilia, I told him he could keep it. He accepted with the degree of incredulous pleasure Pools' Winners reserve for their Littlewoods cheque. Not for the first time in my life, I felt distressingly inadequate.

It would, however, be quite wrong to imply that cricket constantly and exclusively predominates in the island's consciousness. The England pre-Test practice matches received scant attention in the *Daily Gleaner*, Jamaica's officially independent, though if anything pro-opposition, newspaper. Considering a rather embarrassing seven-wicket rout at the hands of the lowly Windward Islands, the region's worst team and bottom of the Shell Shield League, this silence was probably golden. The *Sunday Gleaner* did not even advert to England's performance against the Leeward Islands in Antigua, and only a copy of *The Sunday Times* arriving three days later from London allayed our worst suspicions — that England had been ignominiously defeated. Far more interest and attention has inevitably been focused on Jamaica's performances, and their ultimately thwarted efforts to win the Shell Shield. Ironically, in the match after England's fiasco they too suffered an inglorious defeat at the hands of the much denigrated Windwards.

'Extraordinary amount of rain this season,' Allan Rae, the President of the West Indies Board of Control told me in confidence. 'Very good for the spinners.'

'Why don't you tell that to the England selection committee?' I asked him.

'And why should I of all people do that?' he laughed mischievously.

In early February, however, even Allan's thoughts were directed to much weightier problems than cricket. The neighbouring island of Haiti had been in an *état de siège* for some weeks before the President-for-life dictator, Jean-Claude Duvalier 'Baby Doc' (son of the last President for life 'Papa Doc'), was helped on his way to France, courtesy of the United States air force. Duvalier's governmental mismanagement, the endemic bribery and corruption, the terror tactics of his secret militia — the dreaded Tonton Macoutes — had long been a festering and embarrassing sore, a thorn in the side of the erstwhile supportive American Administration. Mrs Michele Duvalier's well-publicized shopping spree was possibly the multi-million pound straw which broke the American camel's back and the results of U.S. opprobrium finally came swift and fast. Indeed almost too swift and fast. With the extraordinary diplomatic style which the Americans seem to have perfected under Ronnie 'I think Rambo is a helluva good idea for foreign policy' Reagan, an official White House statement announced

Duvalier's departure a full week before it actually happened.

The England team arrived at Kingston airport on the 11th February. Anti-apartheid demonstrations at the airport were limited to half a dozen female students, jumping up and down energetically and generally enjoying themselves in an aerobic sort of way. It was more a vaguely political overspill from the noisy Carnival reaching its climax on the University of West Indies' campus, than anything genuinely unfriendly.

The team's arrival was a full three hours late, due to a technical fault. The plane, it transpired, was missing a bit. The bit was in Trinidad. The plane was in Antigua. We are in the West Indies.

On arrival, Phil went over to the demonstrators, apologized for the unavoidable delay, and thanked them for waiting so patiently. The girls collapsed in giggles. So much for the demo. A police cavalcade mounted on motor bikes escorted the team coach straight to the British High Commissioner's residence, with a reckless disregard for anything even vaguely analogous to the Highway Code — an omni-prevalent attitude in Kingston. As an ex-British colony, Jamaica's motorists drive on the left. Well, occasionally. They stop at red lights too. Occasionally. And occasionally, if a stray hand searching for the radio volume misses the mark, the odd indicator light may inadvertently flash.

The British High Commissioner's cocktail party was a very merry thrash. These dos, on occasions, seem duty-calls for both hosts and guests, to be suffered by both parties rather than enjoyed, but quite the reverse was true in Kingston. The High Commissioner, Martin Reid, and his wife Jane, are a most warm, friendly, hospitable and entertaining couple. A 'highly-placed diplomatic source' (that is to say a mate of mine in the Foreign Office), had telexed ahead, advising them to take cover on my arrival. It is the sort of courtesy world meteorologists extend to one another when Big Bertha is en route. A lifetime in the diplomatic service, however, had

47

inured the Reids to perils manifold, and undaunted they invited me, later, to lunch.

Jane is a keen and well-informed historian, and has produced a booklet on their Residence, Trafalgar House, one of the 15 properties in the whole Foreign and Commonwealth Office's Estate to have been chosen as being of particular historical importance and of architectural merit. Martin is a gifted artist and an Oxford classicist, and we therefore spent a fascinating luncheon discussing common friends and foreign languages. Did you know for instance, that you can still get by in Rumania speaking Latin? The Emperor Trajan gave his faithful troops lands in the region, and the language has continued to flourish in a kind of time warp.

The Third Secretary for Passports and Immigration, drafted into lunch in his capacity as captain of the High Commission cricket team, struggled manfully to bring the conversation around to the Test. That, after all, is what cricket wives are *supposed* to talk about.

To return to the party, however, there Phil and I were reunited, a chaste connubial kiss eliciting quite disproportionately bawdy cheers from one A. Lamb.

The team looked tanned and fit. They also looked very smart, considering their long, hot and sticky travels, in their tour issue grey slacks, blue short-sleeved shirts, and M.C.C. touring ties. The more conservative matrons of Kingston had recently been somewhat less than impressed by the sartorial *laissez-aller* of the Manchester United F.C. manager, Ron Atkinson, at a similar function. Open-neck shirts and large gold medallions nestling on palpitating, hairy chests are not, however, the hallmark of the England cricket team management.

The selection of Tony Brown as tour manager surprised no-one, after his sterling performance on the arduous Indian trip. The choice of R.G.D. Willis as assistant manager has been far more controversial. People have expressed the view that more time should be allowed to elapse before making the transition from player to manager. It is often considered difficult to wield authority over contemporaries and mates, and Allan Lamb has not been slow to christen him T.C. (Turn-Coat). I, preferring to accord him the full status of his three initials, refer to him as P.T.G. (Poacher-Turned-Gamekeeper). Nicknames are, of course, an integral part of the sixth-form mentality, team-spirit ethic. Breakfast at the Pegasus Hotel begins to sound like feeding time at the zoo, with Goose (Willis), Goat (Edmonds), Froggie (French), and Lamby (Lamb), all tucking in.

A tally of the most disparate casualties has begun to accrue. Bruce French, the reserve wicketkeeper, has been bitten in the leg by a dog whilst taking his constitutional run in Antigua. The incident, naturally, gave rise to the greatest concern, but the latest reports suggest that the dog is doing perfectly well. Tim Robinson is complaining of blurred vision, having successfully managed to stuff two contact lenses into each eye. Allan Lamb has been suffering from an irritating growth (a *Pterygium*) near the iris. My brother, the eye surgeon, was prevailed upon to examine them. For the first time in many years I was pleased that he had not elected gynaecology as his speciality.

The usual test of identifying letters from a chart hanging on a wall revealed that poor Robinson, minus contact lenses, experienced great difficulty in locating the wall. Onlookers Edmonds and Lamb were something less than sympathetic. 'Heck,' said Lamb, 'better not tell Number Three!'

A thorough examination revealed no serious damage bar some badly scratched lenses. A complete eye test, however, involved the dilation of Tim's pupil to ensure that nothing was wrong with the back of his eye. The procedure is most disconcerting since the patient's close vision is totally blurred for the subsequent four hours. After the treatment Robinson's pupil was still as large as a saucer, and he was understandably concerned as his thoughts turned to Michael Holding, and a lightning-fast Sabina Park wicket the next day.

Lamb's complaint was fortunately a phenomenon quite

common in people exposed to excessive sunlight, and a course of steroid eye drops would clear it up. Cursory tests, carried out for a lark, revealed quite perfect eyesight in Phil, and a bunch of cataracts in me. I am now a firm believer in the veracity of ignorance being bliss.

Three days later, after a vicious blast of intimidatory bowling from Courtney Walsh in the Jamaica—England match, David Gower too was worried about his eyesight. West Indian policy was obviously to 'psyche' the England captain before the First Test, and even David's most severe critics were obliged to admit that he had been attacked by a pretty unplayable barrage. He went to see my brother, escorted by the team Minder 'Moose', a 6' 5'' 18-stone West Indian detective. I, for one, am really pleased that Moose is on our side. To paraphrase a famous English general, I don't know what he does to the enemy, but he sure scares the wits out of me.

David, it happily transpired, has impeccable vision. He also impressed himself on my brother, as he does on everyone he meets, as a disarmingly charming and intelligent young man. Thus far he had had a pretty nightmarish tour. The psychological effect of his mother dying so soon before the team left for the West Indies has probably not been sufficiently quantified. As an only child, whose father died many years ago, he is probably feeling desperately lonely and bereft. Cricket is so much a question of feeling psychologically 'good', and of trying to establish a firm foothold in the ever shifting sands of that flighty and unfaithful lady, confidence. The vicious circle of loss of confidence—bad form, bad form—loss of confidence is a difficult one to break. David, however, has been through this particularly disheartening mill before, and has emerged triumphant. We are all fervently hoping for his own sake and for the team's, that he soon comes good.

One of the minor casualties, John Emburey, Phil's Middlesex 'Spin-Twin', was in fine fettle at the High Commissioner's party, having completely recovered from a skinned spinning finger. This is a complaint most spinners suffer from, and Phil tries to obviate the worst excesses by frequent annointment with evil-smelling, ubiquitously and indelibly staining Friar's balsam.

The contents of Embers' luggage have occasioned much mirth in the team. His wife, Susie, and new baby, Chlöe, will be joining the team in Barbados, and John has had the forsight to bring a suitcase full of 'Pampers' with him. Pampers, for the benefit of the uninitiated, is a brand of disposable baby nappy. (The term disposable, one assumes, relates primarily to the nappy rather than the baby.) They are an exorbitantly expensive commodity in the Caribbean. 'Cost a lot of money for one crap', as my brother's maid, Ionee, put it neatly, with a scatological delicacy worthy of a gastroenterologist. Yet well may the macho-men of the England team smirk at dear Embers. If this new Jamaican 'quickie' is half as fast as people say, Pampers could soon become an essential addition to the England cricket kit, and Baby Emburey will be left to make out as best she can.

After the party, I spirited Phil off to a local 'Ethiopian' vegetarian restaurant, run by Rastafarians, for a quiet *tête-à-tête* reunion. The Rasta-men's often terrifying appearance, occasioned by the wild and woolly mane of dreadlocks, belies a generally peaceful and godfearing disposition. Indeed, the true Rastafarian desires nothing besides the bare essentials in food and drink, his hair and his Bible. Smoking of the sacramental herb, ganja (marijuana) is an integral part of the Rastafarian cult, but an indulgence which often creates problems with the powers that be.

We had a colourful meal of ackee (a bright yellow vegetable, with the taste, consistency, and appearance of scrambled egg), callaloo (a spicy, green leafy vegetable not unlike spinach), and a generous helping of the West Indian main staple of rice and peas.

We finished our dinner and asked for the bill. The waiter's glazed expression began to exude the vague Jamaican equivalent of 'Nudge-Nudge, Wink-Wink', which perversely involves neither nudges nor winks. Did we want anything, he enquired meaningfully, 'for afters'?

'Why not?' rejoined Edmonds expansively. 'I think I'll have a sorbet'.

Other team-mates, one feels, might not have made so refined a choice.

5

Off the pitch

The kind of 'siege' mentality we saw in India is starting to develop in the team. Some of the players, particularly the 'ex-rebels', feel, quite understandably, under threat. Free time seems to be spent in laager-formation around the pool of the Pegasus, the team's hotel, or at the Liguanea Club over the road, where Mike Gatting has already organized a steak and kidney pudding foray. The British High Commissioner has also generously offered his swimming pool and tennis court to the team. Only a few intrepid souls make it the 20 yards from the Pegasus to the Wyndham Hotel, where the Ristorante d'Amore Italian restaurant is allegedly one of the best in town. The French Ambassador, exhibiting a degree of internationalism not common in Les Français, has said that it purveys truly haute cuisine and, where food is concerned, French Ambassadors usually know best.

Phil is officially 'sharing' a room with Peter Willey. How successive England teams have tolerated this sharing policy for three months at a time with no recorded incidents of homicide ensuing is remarkable indeed. Two large men and four large cricket coffins into one small twin room simply don't go. 'Unofficially', Phil is staying with my brother and me on the campus of the University of the West Indies. Pursuant to T.C.C.B. tour note 126, subparagraph 23, fourth indent (as already mentioned), wives are not encouraged to join their husbands for the first six weeks of the tour. A wife could, presumably, join somebody else's husband, or a husband, could, presumably, invite somebody else's wife, but these are legalistic loopholes no one has ever thought to exploit. Under cover of darkness, I spirit Phil away from the hotel in the evening and ferry him back in the morning at 6.30 am.

At 34 and 33 respectively, I cannot help but feel that Phil and I are getting a bit old for this illicit midnight tryst sort of business. At least Peter Willey, not a man given to excesses of emotion, seems relatively content with the arrangement. The restricted periods Phil spends in the room are devoted to complaining about Peter's air-conditioning setting, scrounging his shampoo, borrowing his swimming trunks, and changing any TV programme he happens to be watching. Peter maintains an air of pained patience.

The University is, however, a far more interesting place to be at the moment than any faceless, intercontinental hotel. The present Prime Minister, Edward Seaga, is more or less of the Margaret Thatcher School of Economics, and the last few years have witnessed swingeing cuts in public works, social services, education and health care. Incidents of malnutrition, never witnessed under the more charismatic, caring, if often economically profligate socialist Michael Manley, are beginning to crop up with monotonous and worrying regularity at the University Hospital. Members of the hospital staff who have tried to bring the disturbing facts and statistics to public attention have been warned to watch their step. The Kingston equivalent of the Greater London Council has been summarily disbanded, though to be fair many people have alleged that it was riddled with corruption, irresponsible expenditure, and a number of paid employees who were not exactly still in the land of the living. *Plus ça change* . . .

The teachers are also currently on strike, complaining of pitiful pay, and ridiculously bad teacher to pupil ratios. In this general climate of budgetary restraint and economic austerity, the University lecturers were pleasantly staggered when their salary and allowance demands were accommodated immediately. Divide and conquer! A few weeks later the government decided to introduce an economic fee for university students. One of the tenets of Manley's administration had always been free education for all.

'Michael would shout "free education", to the wild acclaim of his adoring supporters,' one University professor told me. 'And then, with a glorious disregard for the financial consequences he would turn to his Education Minister, visibly on the brink of a coronary, and say, "Now *you* organize it".'

Until this year, students were obliged to pay a token fee, some J$100 (about £14) per annum, patently not an economic fee. However, overnight, the Seaga Government has increased the fees to J$5,000 for Natural Sciences and Law, and to J$6,000 for Medicine and Engineering. Student demonstrations inevitably ensued, and the university is still barricaded off. Average parents do not have that kind of money, and many, indeed most, students will be obliged to quit their studies mid-stream.

Children of affluent parents, *les petits fils de papa*, the only students who will be able to continue their Law or Medical studies, are certainly not the sort to stay subsequently in Jamaica to ply their respective trades. They will be off to the States or to the U.K. where the pickings are richer. And thus the whole reason for the foundation of the University of the West Indies in 1948, to produce some home grown West Indian doctors, lawyers and engineers is gradually being thwarted.

It would, however, be unfair to paint too black a picture of the Seaga Government. What you do not have, as every housewife or grocer's daughter will tell you, you simply cannot spend. The pro-Marxist Manley administration left the Jamaican economy in ruins. 'Spend, spend, spend' may well be a popular and populist policy, but eventually quarter-day arrives. There had been a massive efflux of god-and-communist-fearing American capital under Manley, and the economic *et, tu, Brute?* came in the form of a dramatic fall in the world price of bauxite: Jamaica is the world's largest producer of bauxite, an iron-rich mineral which is used in the manufacture of aluminium.

The general post-oil-price-hike world recession also hit Jamaica very badly in the 1970s, and the tourist industry collapsed as stories of Jamaican street violence and shoot-outs percolated abroad. Seaga has therefore had his work cut out to put Jamaica back on the 'safe and civilized' map after his resounding electoral victory in 1980. Seaga's most vehement critics may well be justified in criticizing him for acting more often in the interests of the International Monetary Fund than of the Jamaican people, but he who pays the political fiddler calls the economic tune. Confidence is gradually being restored in Jamaica, and the American Caribbean Basin Initiative (C.B.I.) is certainly helping to create wealth and jobs in a country where 30 per cent unemployment is considered to be a conservative estimate of a fairly insoluble problem.

In 1982, when the number of young people unemployed reached the alarming statistic of 80,000 (80,000 young people, between the ages of 17—24 unemployed, out of a total population of 2.2 million is a potentially inflammable caucus indeed), the Prime Minister himself set up the H.E.A.R.T. (Human Employment And Resource Training) programme. It is vaguely analogous to British Youth Training Schemes, except that instead of being government funded, it is financed entirely out of the private sector. All companies over a certain size are obliged to 'donate' three per cent of their wage-bill to the scheme. Should the company take on a H.E.A.R.T. trainee, the trainee's salary of J$50 per week is deducted from the overall donation. Companies' donation records are extremely good. Failure to come up with the goods generally results in suspension of a trading, or import—export licence. In Jamaica, they have ways of making you pay.

I visited the H.E.A.R.T. Trust, and was impressed to hear a plethora of statistics on the numbers of young people who had graduated successfully from Cosmetology, Agricultural,

Building, Crafts, and Textiles Courses. No one, however, would supply me with the one statistic I really wanted to know. How many of these young people actually end up with a job? The government has also embarked on an ambitious 'Solidarity' scheme, designed to set young school leavers up in their own small businesses: usually ice-cream, or 'Jerk' pork and chicken outlets. Job improvement policies have also been implemented, although these are more often nominal than substantial. The ubiquitous pedlars, or 'higglers', must now, officially, be referred to as 'I.C.I.s', (Informal Commercial Importers): whereas my old man was once a dustman, he is now a sanitary inspector.

Despite official unemployment figures of 25 per cent, however (the true figure is probably in the region of 35 per cent), and a rate of inflation running at some 30 per cent, Jamaica would seem on a more even keel than outsiders are often led to believe. Prime Minister Seaga was recently infuriated by a report drawn up by the United States' political risk analysts, Frost and Sullivan, concluding that violent unrest was fomenting in Jamaica, and that the situation could well be further exacerbated in 1986. Professor Gladstone Mills, Professor of Public Administration at the University of the West Indies (and also incidentally a member of the Jamaican Cricket Board of Control dealing with press relations) felt the report was based on a total misunderstanding of a survey commissioned by the University of West Indies itself, and certainly many of the conclusions drawn were not predicated on absolute fact.

Certainly, to an observant outsider, the man in the Old Hope Road, Kingston does not seem to be teetering on the brink of civil war. And to be fair to the Seaga government, certain classic economic indicators look very positive indeed. The Stock Market, for example, has quadrupled in the last three years from an index of 240 at the end of December 1983, to an index of 900 in February 1986. Even taking into account a 30 per cent inflation rate, this represents a doubling in real terms.

Economics, however, as my Bank Manager will readily concur, has never been my forte. I therefore asked a Financial Economist working for the British Government, and amongst other things researching into this phenomenon, what it could all mean. Did it, I asked, trying with difficulty to look intelligent and 'meaningful', did it mean greater international confidence in the government; did it mean real growth in the economy; did it mean increased overseas investment; or did it mean more disposable income?

'Dunno,' he answered, in a British Government sort of way, the authority of three years' research under his belt. 'I think it means the Jamaicans like a casino.'

Inveterate gamblers indeed, the Jamaicans knew where to put their money when it came to cricket.

6

On the pitch

Today I decided to go and watch my husband bat. This does not usually involve much, if any, time, and so I had organized an early lunch at the Liguanea Club with Adrian Murrell. Adrian has kindly agreed to do all the pictures for this book and is universally acclaimed as one of the best sports photographers in the business.

Phil had forgotten that it was Valentine's Day, and so one of the team's liaison officers, Stafford Shann, was swiftly despatched to purchase a card for me. Phil had also forgotten his wallet, so Stafford had to pay for it. And Phil had forgotten his pen, so Stafford had to sign it. Phil also had to race off to the cricket (he had forgotten he was still batting), so Stafford had to deliver it. It really can be overwhelming, being married to such an incurable romantic!

I met Geoff Boycott waiting in the lobby of the Pegasus Hotel. I am always thoroughly pleased to see him and he must figure as one of my all time favourite people on the cricket circuit. He has constantly been a loyal and supportive friend to both Phil and me, and on more than one occasion has incurred the wrath of the T.C.C.B. gods for criticizing Phil's exclusion from successive touring parties. He is covering the tour as *The Mail on Sunday's* correspondent, but has brought his cricket kit with him as well as his typewriter. He can often be located during the course of the day having a net at Sabina Park, and there is intense, if officially groundless, speculation that Geoff's talents as an opening batsman may once more be required should the England batting disintegrate. They could do a lot worse than Sir Geoffrey.

We had all been suffering from the most vicious attacks of mosquito bites. Despite prophylactic rubbing with *Autan* and remedial rubbing with *Anthisan*, the topography of my legs still resembled one of the blacker, more mogul-ridden pistes at Gstaadt.

'Don't worry,' said Geoff soothingly, 'they only attack fertile women.'

I was, in my leprous condition, suitably pleased to hear this.

'Conceived in Jamaica, born in Melbourne,' mused Geoff hermetically.

It is sometimes difficult, even for a Cheshire lass, to follow the labyrinths of a Yorkshire mind.

'Next tour's to Australia,' explained Phil, laconically.

'Could be,' I said, 'but you are not going . . .'

I spent the morning watching the cricket from the Press Box at Sabina Park. Compliance with certain rules in the Box is absolutely mandatory, and these were explained to me by Scyld Berry, the cricket correspondent of *The Observer*.

1. No laughing.
2. No applauding.
3. No enjoying yourself.
4. On the hour, every hour, complain loudly about:
   a) the telephones
   b) the telex system
   c) the locals
   d) 'abroad'
   e) the telephones . . .

The first person I came across was Peter Smith of the *Daily Mail*, who did not appear to be excessively conversant with any of the rules. He welcomed me into the 'holy of holies' with a wide toothy grin. Toothy, unfortunately, involved just one front tooth, since Peter had lost the other one in an altercation with a step in Antigua. He had been putting it religiously under his pillow every night, and waiting for the *Mail* fairy to cough up the impending damage. Poor Peter.

The tooth was eventually fixed, but the fairy never came.

Sitting just in front of me was Scyld. It was, after all, St Valentine's Day, and Scyld had retrieved two pictures of his wife from the hotel safe that morning. He spent a large part of the first session mooning over them. Not your typical hard-nosed hack, our Scyld. The reverie was broken by whoops of glee from Matthew Engel, *The Guardian* correspondent. His phone had rung! The day before, the telephones had duly been installed, but the attendant wires unfortunately led nowhere. During the course of the night, however, somebody had patently attached them to something, and hence Matthew's undisguised delight at the first telephonic tinkle.

'It's for you, Scyld,' he reported a minute later, a trifle put out. 'The woman from the Tourist Office about the trip to Negril.'

From the front of the box rang the mellifluous and patrician tones of Christopher Martin-Jenkins, commentating on the match for listeners of the BBC at home in England. Christopher has been the unfortunate recipient of two death threats. Surely *The Cricketer* magazine, of which he is editor, cannot be *that* provocative. It seems an innocuous enough publication. And Christopher himself is the mildest-mannered and most inoffensive of men.

'I am sorry to hear about the appalling weather you are having back home,' Christopher was saying. 'Sorry to rub it in, but it really is the most glorious day here at Sabina Park.'

It suddenly struck me in a blinding flash of incandescent lucidity: the death threats were more than likely from some hypothermic crank snowed up in deepest Derbyshire!

The excitement of the cricket was all a bit too much to with-stand, and the next day I went off to Negril. If one of the world's best sports photographers and one of England's top cricket correspondents felt that they could waltz off with impunity, I certainly saw no good reason to stick around. Phil, incidentally, carried his bat manfully in the first innings, bowled very well in the second, and England won the match. Anyone who, four months later, cares to know further details of this perfectly turgid game, should turn to the back of this book and consult a good psychiatrist.

We flew to Negril in a tiny Cessna 206, just large enough to accommodate four passengers and the pilot. The pilot swept low over illicit but uncontrollable ganja plantations. These are usually located in perfectly inacessible spots, far removed from roads or even tracks, and virtually impossible to police. There is far too much money riding on this lowly, 'sacramental' herb for it to be successfully stamped out. It was said by some influential politicians that ganja was one of the 'mainstays' of their economy.

In a country where poverty is rife, and proprietary medicines are both excessively expensive and often unobtainable, infusions of ganja are drunk for medicinal purposes, and ointments and balms of the herb are used to soothe and heal. Smoking the stuff is an integral part of the Rastafarian culture and religious belief and a lot of West Indians will tell you that it is certainly not as deleterious to your health as tobacco, or alcohol. Against a groundswell of popular beliefs such as these, the government certainly has a Sisyphean task on its hands in trying to mobilize public opinion against the drug.

'While there's ganja and fire', said the captain of our snorkelling boat, expertly smoking the stuff out of a pipe formed from his own bare, cupped hands, 'oh, man, while there's ganja and fire, no one gonna stop us from smokin' it.' My companions and I nodded politely and sympathetically, as he waved his harpoon-gun at us for suitable dramatic effect.

The American tourists, in particular, are quick to exploit the ubiquitous and readily available nature of the local dope. Stories abound of holiday paradises such as 'Hedonism II', where naked strangers cavort merrily together, thrashing around in the warm intimacy of the jacuzzi, and knocking back banana daiquiris, high as kites on ganja. Paul 'SHOCK HORROR PHEW WHAT A SCORCHER' Weaver, of the

News of the World, (but now of *The Mirror*), decided to go there for a bit of 'investigative journalism' during one of the rest days. He was not a little disconcerted on arrival, however, to find a well supported egg-and-spoon-race in progress, and lots of Americans heavily into nothing more noxious than waffles.

People in the Jamaican Tourist industry are, however, most disturbed at the paucity of English tourists to the island. The Americans, on the contrary, arrive in droves. It is a mere 90-minute hop from Miami to Montego Bay, and they are much in evidence at all the resorts along the north coast. We took the compulsory tourist trip to Rick's Café on the westernmost promontory of Negril in order to see the sunset. It was a genuinely magnificent sight, as the incandescent reds and oranges disintegrated into a tiny mercurial blob, and suddenly disappeared into a restless blue-black sea. To a man, the Americans broke into a round of spontaneous applause. Helios, no doubt, will be pleased that Uncle Sam approves his act.

While we were away, England managed to defeat Jamaica, a much needed psychological fillip, despite the fact that the Jamaicans had not unleashed their new, fast, wonder-weapon, Patrick Patterson. The worst was yet to come.

Sabina Park is not so romantic a cricket ground as a superficial description would perhaps lead one to believe. It is true you can see the Carribbean, sapphire blue in the distance, and that the glorious Blue Mountains, world famous for their coffee, are also much in evidence. The profusion of barbed wire and wire netting are not, however, the sort of precautions one would need to stay even the wildest excesses of the 'Egg and Bacon' brigade at Lord's. And the ratio of one member of the Jamaica Constabulary Force per five spectators seems a little on the high side. They are a handsome bunch of men, these members of the J.C.F., most striking in their black jodphurs, set off to great effect by a thick red stripe down the side. The *pièce de résistance* is a red and black cummerbund, bejewelled with silver buckle. One wag assured me that the basic criterion for entry into the force, and in order to ensure correct deportment in this very natty uniform, was possession of a 23-inch waist. Possession of an I.Q. in a similar statistical region is not entirely disadvantageous either.

Juxtaposed with this indubitable sartorial splendour is quite a frightening array of riot equipment: batons, rifles, and Smith and Wesson tear gas canisters. I was beginning to feel that the likes of Siegfried Sassoon should be in the Press Box to chronicle the ensuing trench-warfare. It was, therefore, a relief to learn that the full riot gear, tear-gas and all, had only ever been used on one occasion, when unfortunately the male-model J.C.F.'s failed to take into account details such as wind-direction, and the egregious incumbents of the Governor-General's and Prime Minister's boxes were felled in lachrymose and angry heaps.

Today, however, the mood in Sabina Park is carnival. There have been a few token demonstrations outside the ground, but nothing of moment. Certainly, I have seen more aggressive West Indian contingents at the Surrey Oval than at Kingston Sabina. It may be that the West Indian faction here doesn't feel as socially oppressed as their counterparts in England. Yet, nevertheless, although the crowd is here to watch and enjoy their cricket, one felt that it is black supremacy that has drawn them. It is the very argument that many West Indians, including Viv Richards, have used in pleading for the tour to go ahead: 'We are the best in the world. Now give us the chance to prove it'.

For me the One-day International was a combination of tedium and horror, the unremitting onslaught of the West Indian four-pronged pace attack (Garner, Patterson, Marshall, and Holding) and the efforts of a struggling England batting line-up merely to survive. 'A bit like bear-baiting,' remarked Simon Barnes of *The Times*, 'only we're on the side of the bears'.

It is perfectly obvious that if England possessed the same

phalanx of fast bowlers, they would indubitably use them to the same effect. What I am saying is not meant as a criticism of the brilliantly indomitable West Indian bowling machine. It is quite simply that I, as a non-purist, fail to see the 'poetry-in-motion' of fast bowlers smashing people to pieces. It is for the same reasons that even as a total hispanophile, I cannot betake myself to the *Corrida*, the bullfight, the Spanish national sport.

A good *corrida* is, I am told, a pure art form: dramatic theatre at its highest level. A good *matador* is a combination of actor, dancer, and executioner. At a poetic and metaphorical level he represents man's struggle and final victory over the forces of evil. With bull-fighting, as with intimidatory cricket, I *do* understand that the aficionados derive much aesthetic pleasure, enjoyment, and excitement from the contest, but it is, quite frankly, the kind of buzz I personally can live without. Moreover, this is the sort of sport which, though appealing to the aesthetic values of the true purists, more often appeals to the basest, most animal instincts of the masses: that far from admirable quality of blood-lust.

Sorry for getting a bit heavy. The only point I wish to make is that this is not the kind of cricket I like to watch. Apart from anything else it puts me off my gin and tonic, especially when my own husband is nearly killed. But more of that later.

The first major casualty on this tour was Mike Gatting. It is always reassuring to see Mike's stocky, squarish frame make its way out to the crease. Once again, Robinson and Gower had failed to make many runs. Poor David. Uneasy, indeed, lies the head that wears the crown. He looked so slim and frail and wispish, like a pedigree two-year-old filly, as he walked disconsolately back to his team-mates in the dressing-room. 'Gatt', on the contrary, is vaguely reminiscent of a shire horse. Strong, sturdy, reliable, unflappable, he walked out to the wicket swinging his bat, doing his little on-the-spot-running hops, and looking decidedly as if he, at least, meant business.

Ten runs later he was writhing on the ground in a pool of his own blood, hit in the face by a ball from Malcolm Marshall. He was helped off the field, his nose completely broken and flattened, his face totally unrecognizable. They tell us Joel Garner subsequently found a piece of bone, a quarter of an inch long, embedded in the ball. I left for home, feeling perfectly sick, and wondering whether it was my place to phone his wife, Elaine, in London, to tell her what had happened before she saw it on the news. Fortunately, the manager, Tony Brown, a very considerate and thoughtful man, had done the unpleasant necessary.

A West Indian lawyer friend of ours, Ferdie Johnson, rushed Gatt off to hospital, helped by Ian Botham, who was not playing in that match due to injury.

'I could not have been more impressed with "Both",' Ferdie told me later. 'He kept trying to keep Gatt's spirits up, laughing and joking all the time. "Come on Gatt," he said, ribbing him, "it's happened to all of us, it's about time it happened to you." '

After Botham's incredible marathon from John o'Groats to Land's End, many people are beginning to believe that beneath this ultra-macho, devil-may-care image, there probably is a heart of 22 carat gold. It would be tragic indeed to think that unless someone, either inside or outside the team, musters the guts, the authority and the discipline to channel his terrible talents and energies, then we may well witness another 'George Best' phenomenon. Certainly, it would appear to be highly deleterious to team spirit to have one superstar who cannot be bothered to practise, or condescend to play in regional 'warm-up' games. A desire to appear, *deus ex machina*, for the 'big one' is fine, so long as your arrival centre-stage changes the course of proceedings. So far we have not seen much evidence of this, but with Both you never know . . .

To his credit he does not appear to harbour a grudge, despite a pen-portrait I adumbrated for the *Daily Express*, describing him as 'in no way inhibited by a capacity to overintellectualize'. It is exactly the sort of thing I would say to his face, and I'm convinced even Both himself would be inclined to agree with it.

Consigning such comments to a daily newspaper is probably not, however, the way to make friends and influence people. Other team-mates are not quite so forgiving or forgetting. Certain players, quite rightly, view me with a great deal of suspicion after my minor flirtations with the press and limited excursions into journalism. It probably would have been easier, in retrospect, to describe them all in the terms they want to hear: 'Tall, dark, handsome, intelligent, charming, polished, witty, urbane . . .' but that would probably have precipitated several successful libel suits. In any event, I am currently paying the price for my literary transgressions, and feel suitably devastated to be emarginalized *ad eternum* from the incandescent wit and wisdom of at least two of the England squad.

England, needless to say, was decisively beaten in the first One-day International, and the worst aspects of the British gutter press began to rear their ugly heads. The depths to which certain sordid sleuths will stoop are certainly abysmal. Why newspapers cannot simply accept that players are out of form, or professionally incapable of dealing with this unstoppable West Indian barrage is beyond me. The absolute pits, we all felt, was reached when the wife of one member of the team was telephoned and asked 'whether there was any truth in the rumour' that she was having an affair with another member of the team, thus explaining his loss of form. It is classic *Private Eye* stuff. A flat denial will, in any event, elicit a headline 'Mrs X denies rumours of affair with Mr Y'. It is the sort of gutter-game you just cannot win.

Relations between the team and the press are always a love-hate affair. I have yet to meet any cricketer who does not welcome the adulation and enjoy the indubitable privileges which media coverage generally bestows. When England is doing well, and the press is busily filing laudatory encomiums of often quite excessive and unctuous praise, then the player-press boat seems to rock along quite smoothly. When the team is failing badly, however, the media worm inevitably turns, and many a player's hubris and carefully massaged ego is loath to take the slightest hint of personal criticism. It is then that the affair turns sour.

Many of the press have commented to me on their exclusion from official functions and extra-mural activities on this tour, something which never happened last year in India. Many are wont to blame the assistant manager, Bob Willis, whose attitude to the press while England captain was always one informed with the deepest suspicion. 'Big Bob', however, demonstrates feelings common to about ninety-nine per cent of players, and if exclusions either perceived or real are down to him, his actions would no doubt be welcomed by the majority of the team.

Phil, on the contrary, has always actively sought the company of many members of the press corps. They are, by and large, far more expansive, entertaining and rounded company than professional cricketers, and Phil must be one of the few players who actually invites *them* to dinner. With the exception of a few really pernicious and ultimately very dangerous characters, the cricket press are a very decent bunch, and I say that, despite the generous dollops of aggro they have ladled out to Phil in the past. What they write about the team is sometimes bad enough, but what they know and do not write often demonstrates the discretion of the innermost sanctuary of the Curia. Most of them are not, at least, in the business of breaking up marriages.

It would, however, be perfectly wrong to suggest that the team's entire time is spent parrying either the West Indian fast bowlers or the English press corps. I cannot speak for all players, some of whose social horizons seem to stretch little further than the team-room or the bar, and whose conversation only seems to sparkle when there is nookey in the offing. But for those who wish to involve themselves in more substantial relationships, there are life-long friendships to be forged on tour.

The Rousseau family, for example, took Phil and me to their hearts and showered us with the most overwhelming kindness, generosity and hospitality. Patrick Rousseau, of the Jamaican Board of Control, and his brother Peter, are two of Jamaica's leading entrepreneurs, with interests in real estate, stud farming and the hotel and restaurant business. One of their restaurants, 'The Blue Mountain Inn' in Kingston, is billed quite correctly as one of the most romantic hostelries on the island, with the backdrop of the Blue Mountains, and the gurgling of the swift-moving mountain stream running through the garden responsible for many a precipitate proposal of marriage. The *Maître d'Hôtel* is an hysterically funny Welshman, Michael Byrne, who fell in love with Jamaica 25 years ago, and gave up his lucrative job designing jewellery for Christian Dior in London to come and live here.

'But, darling,' he confided to me confidentially, 'since I left C.D., it's all tat. Tat. Tat. Tat.' He did not strike me as the rugby-playing sort of Welshman.

The cuisine in the restaurant is eclectic, combining the best in local produce with traditional Jamaican recipes, with less spicy European cooking for the more unadventurous tourists, and a straight sirloin or fillet steak for the Americans. But it seems a sin to me to come to the tropical island paradise of Jamaica to eat imported beef. Why not try a nasal-passage clearing 'Pepperpot' soup, just the sort of thing to make you bowl at 90 miles per hour? Or Jamaica's national dish, Ackee, which mixed together with a bit of fried bacon and smothered over a light pastry base produces a rather exotic Quiche Lorraine. Red-pea soup is another favourite. Strange how people in hot climates feel the need for hot spicy food — I noticed the same phenomenon in India. For the weak in gut and spirit, however, there is always chilled ChoCho soup, a rather nondescript green vegetable rather like a cucumber, which together with a dash of cream and a hint of spice liquidizes into a delicious starter.

For fish-fanciers, smoked marlin — a paler version of smoked salmon served quite simply with onions and capers — is a must. Dolphin (no, not the our friend Flipper variety) and Red Snapper also make frequent appearances on Jamaican menus, but I never miss an opportunity to indulge myself on Caribbean spiny lobster. These are salt water creatures and, unlike other varieties, there is no huge claw: the meat is all in the body. This happily circumvents an awful lot of messy eating. I have oftcn thought that it ill-behoves the elegant lady gourmet to spend hours with a knitting-needle, poking up some defunct crustacean's legs. The detritus of a lady's plate should not look like a road accident. Reverend Mother Paul, Order of St Ursuline, told me that.

The luxuriant profusion of local fruit leaves one with an *embarras de choix*. My favourite is bright orange paw-paw (or papaya), sprinkled with a dash of lime. Water melon of sacerdotal red studded with dark black pips is gloriously refreshing and, for the weight watchers amongst us, of negligible calorific value. Tangerines are huge and the grapefruits are sweet. Bananas abound, and plantains (brothers of bananas), are commonly boiled and served as vegetables. I cannot help it, however, if, as the sister of a consultant gastroenterologist they suggest to me so many anaemic little turds; though comments like that, I'm aware, will never land me Egon Ronay's job.

Imported wine can be found in Jamaica — at a price. All luxury imports are subject to heavy duty. Local wine is, however, available, manufactured on the island from imported grape must. Montpelier Rouge, Pica Rosé, sparkling 'Cold Duck', and very cold Monterey white are all perfectly reasonable and potable brews. Most people, however, drink the local rum, or the increasingly popular local lager, Red Stripe. I refuse, however, to drink anything which does not have a bright green paper umbrella, and a large red maraschino cherry in it. We are, after all, in the Caribbean.

The Rousseau brothers invited us to a very jolly dinner party at the Blue Mountain Inn where I met Raman Subba Row, President of the T.C.C.B., and his wife, Ann, and Bernie Coleman of the T.C.C.B. who deals with promotion. I sometimes find it hard to rationalize my own ambiguous feelings to male-dominated institutions and establishments; to last bastions of male-chauvinist piggery such as the T.C.C.B. and the M.C.C. Although I rail against some of the perfectly ridiculous rules and regulations they waste their time promulgating and, although they are essentially and manifestly anti-feminist in their outlook, I never fail to be completely bowled over by many of their component members. Raman is one of the most refined and charming gentlemen one could ever wish to meet. And darling Bernie is warmly avuncular, generous and kind. Perhaps I should stop waging other women's wars, stop berating committee members about the absence of baby-changing facilities at Lord's, stop criticizing the T.C.C.B. for not subsidizing wives' trips on tour. When all is said and done, I don't actually have a baby to change, and here I am tripping around quite nicely on tour.

And yet the daughters of Emily Pankhurst must fight on. If the individual members of these often insensitive institutions can be so uncompromisingly 'nice', there is no earthly reason why the corporate body cannot be made to wear a more human face.

7

Jamaica and Eden II

The first Test match was a pretty shambolic affair, although a manful, Brian Close-ian second innings from one P.H. Edmonds avoided the unutterable indignity of an innings defeat. There are silver linings to every cloud, however, and the debutant performance of Greg 'Blodwen' Thomas, our new Welsh fast-bowling hope, must surely rate as one of them. Peter Willey also got his head down in the second innings, and taught a useful lesson in patience and obduracy to some of our more elegant batsmen. Richard Ellison, too, bowled particularly well. It must, however, be a dishearteningly Herculean task to attack some of the best batting in the world with a mere 150 runs on the board.

'If England are going to win Test matches, they have got to score some runs,' commented Phil philosophically. I sometimes wonder whether with such profoundly brilliant banalities, he is after David Coleman's job. Allan Lamb and Graham Gooch are also withstanding this fulminating West Indian pace-attack better than most. Phil was extremely impressed with 'Lamby's' determination to succeed, and the hours he puts in practising with the team bowling machine 'Fred'.

Fred is fast becoming a personality in his own right. On the team's day off in Ocho Rios, our local police security men wanted to know if we had brought Fred with us for the ride, such is the extent of his fame and popularity. Fred, in his mere mechanical manifestation, is in fact a BOWLA machine manufactured by Stuart and Williams of Bristol, and is capable of sending down deliveries up to a speed of 90 miles per hour, while getting the ball to swing in or out. He can also spin the ball or deliver bouncers.

Phil suffered the crass indignity on the second day of the tour to mistime a fast one from Fred and to catch it straight in the unmentionables. (Unmentionables incidentally for all ex-convent girl readers, are what we would call 'goolies'.) I phoned him as soon as I heard this gem on the World Service (honestly, you would think the World Service had more cosmically important things to talk about than Edmonds' balls), in order to establish whether the *Bijoux de la Famille* and the Edmonds lineage were safe. Banjaxed cricketers can always be recycled, in any event. If the worst came to the worst yesterday's Phil Edmonds could always be tomorrow's Aled Jones. I was relieved, nevertheless, to hear his dulcet Zambian tones pitched more or less in the right register, and to ascertain that there was nothing wrong with Phil: 'Could I please inspect his injury insurance policy,' he wondered, 'and establish whether compensation was payable on a temporarily disabled "percy" '.

Graham Gooch is faring far better than anyone else against this blistering West Indian bowling, and yet Phil maintains that he has yet to demonstrate that authoritative and masterful stroke-play which so hall-marks his normal batting. It is difficult to assess the psychological effect that all the political fuss and pressure have had on the team in general and Gooch in particular. It must be very disturbing and distracting to be the epicentre of the West Indian anti-apartheid storm. It cannot be very pleasant either to read the comments of such folk-heroes as the ex-Jamaican Prime Minister, Michael Manley.

In a well constructed letter to the *Trinidad Express*, Manley argued forcibly against the abandonment of the tour, but speaks, nevertheless, about his 'lingering indignation about Gooch'. It is unfortunate that Graham Gooch seems to have focused far more flak on himself than any of the other so-called 'Rebels', or 'Rebs' as the rest of the team not unaffectionately call them. The reason is, as Manley further complains, that 'Graham Gooch complicated the matter with a remark contained in a book which he wrote and a statement which he made in a radio interview after he had served his sentence. Understandably and properly there was an outburst including protests from the Government of Antigua which were public, and equally vigorous protests from all other governments at a private level.'

The Deputy Prime Minister of Antigua, Lester Bird, followed up the attack, crowing ornithologically about the so-called 'Gooch Apology', and stating in an open letter (in *The Antigua and Barbuda Herald* of 11th Febraury) his reasons for boycotting the cricket.

By the time the team had reached Jamaica, many of them were heartily sick of being used as white pawns in the Caribbean party-politics chess game. Gooch, in particular, had been wound up by certain members of the not-entirely-responsible press, and indicated to Tony Brown his intention of making yet another statement. Tony asked Phil for his views, and Phil's views were absolutely dogmatic. His understanding of the gist of Gooch's imminent statement was that Gooch felt he had been totally misrepresented with regard to South Africa.

The upshot of such a statement, if ever made public, would have surely been the swift and irretrievable end to the entire tour, and possibly an irredeemable cleavage between English and West Indian cricket. Tony and Phil concurred. Statement-making was not the business of individual players, and should be left entirely to the management. After all, even the White House under Reagan has not yet entrusted diplomatic relations to Joan Rivers.

Phil himself was the centre of a great deal of controversy in the English press over allegedly 'sledging' Gordon Greenidge in the First Test. Sledging, for the uninitiated, involves standing very close to someone and aggravating them to pieces until they feel like hitting you over the head with a cricket bat. Phil does it to me all the time, but I, unfortunately, cannot go and whinge to Viv Richards.

I asked Phil afterwards why on earth he does it, what he

thinks there is to gain out of putting his life on the line fielding in this 'suicide position', picking up catches which do nothing other than improve other people's averages. (*Esprit de corps* was never my forte at school.) 'Well,' said Phil laconically, 'nothing was happening. No one was doing anything. Nobody was taking charge. Gordon was getting his eye in, so I thought I'd go and field a bit closer and put him off his stroke. Besides, I was getting bored.' I often think that man would rather hang off a cliff by his fingernails than run the risk of being bored.

His come-uppance came swiftly, however, at about 90 miles per hour, to be exact. Patrick Patterson, the new greased-lightning Jamaican quickie, unleashed a beamer at Phil, no doubt in his impatience to wind up the Test match, and smacked him straight on the heart. I was totally aghast in a flurry of confusion and panic. How to pop a bottle of Veuve Cliquot, phone the insurance company, and order an extra-large humidor to crate him home all at once? Oh, and something in the old boot for that dear boy, Patrick . . .

Too soon. Edmonds rose slowly, indeed a little perversely, phoenix-like from the dust. There is a protective bodice, a lot of very thick skin, quite a bit of excess adipose tissue and a wodge of cheque books to penetrate before anyone gets anywhere near Phil Edmonds' heart.

The Test was all over and in a mere three days, and the day after the Test Match was, in any case, a 'rest day'. The team, contrary to popular wisdom, does not get very many free days. When they are not playing in regional matches, One-day Internationals and Test Matches they are usually having 'naughty boy' nets, for being naughty boys in regional matches, One-day Internationals and Test Matches. Honestly, it's not all pina coladas and palm trees out here, you know. Nor even, more ethnically, Red Stripes and dominoes. Not that anyone was complaining. The only complaints about this four-pronged, mean-machine West Indian pace attack were in the English press. The boys themselves, believe it or not, did not complain. There were no whingeing Poms in this squad.

The free day after the first Test was therefore spent enjoying some well earned rest and recuperation in Ocho Rios. Who knows? If we could continue to wind up Test matches in three days, there might be more generous helpings of 'R & R' as the tour progresses.

The 24 hours 'off' was spent at Eden II, a day's respite far removed from the pressures of West Indian politics and the barrage of West Indian bowling. Phil and I had stayed in Eden II, after Jamaica Cricket Festival Week the previous October (two cynical, married-ten-years serpents in an American newly-weds' paradise), and we had promised the managing director, an Englishman, Michael Durkin, to take the team there for the rest day if the England management agreed.

Eden II is a staggeringly beautiful all-inclusive couples resort. Only heterosexual couples are allowed to book in — no singles or threesomes. The director waived this rule to accommodate the team for one night, with only a few minor attendant problems. The boys shared rooms, as usual, and we did have a few domestic squabbles the next morning as to who would get the Eden II 'His' tee-shirt, and who would be left with the 'Hers'. Some of them had inadvertently hit the bed vibrator button before switching off the lights, and had sensational nights dreaming of the earth moving. They have ways of making the earth move for everybody at Eden II.

This all-inclusive concept is along the lines of Club Mediterranée idea, and very popular with American tourists to Jamaica. For the equivalent of around £1,000 per week (depending on the season), a couple is provided with the most delightfully decorated room and balcony; all meals; all drinks (that's the dangerous one); constant snacks; all water-sports including water skiing, wind-surfing, scuba diving, snorkeling, sailing and lessons in how to do them; horseback riding; entertainment and disco dancing . . . the list is endless.

The team spent most of the day relaxing by the sea, enjoying the water sports. The waiters were agog to have them there. Eden II had just won the Ocho Rios hotel cricket league, and the power and build of their three fast bowlers led one to the inevitably distressing conclusion that there are far more where Patrick Patterson came from. The hospitality of the house was extended to us for another night if we wished, but we were obliged to race back to Kingston. After all, the team had just lost the Test Match in three days, and the next day was the inexorable naughty boy nets.

Patrick Eagar and Adrian Murrell, two of the photographers, stayed behind, however. Poor Adrian and Patrick. They got some unfairly funny looks when they tipped up for breakfast the next morning: two male photographers, and 263 nice normal heterosexual couples.

The sands of time were running out swiftly in Jamaica. Everyone was beginning to feel that this could well be the best leg of the tour. Disturbing rumours of 5,000 anti-apartheid demonstrators walking through the Trinidadian capital, Port of Spain, waving 'England Team, Go Home' placards, made us feel that we could do a lot worse than stay on in the Pegasus Hotel, Kingston.

On our last day, Phil and I were invited to visit the Jamaica Tobacco Company to learn about the manufacture of Royal Jamaica cigars. Phil has been watching far too many Carmen films, and listening to far too many tales about cigars being rolled on maidens' inner thighs, and accepted the invitation with alacrity. He was not a little disappointed to ascertain that the Trades Description Act obtains in Jamaica, too, and hand-made cigars means just that.

The company is family owned and run by the two Gore brothers, Phillip and Robert, substantial Jamaican entrepreneurs. The company has been exporting cigars since 1939, principally to the United States of America, Australia, the United Kingdom and the Federal Republic of Germany. The Managing Director, Robert, told us that the company was organizing a new marketing thrust in Europe. Spain, which acceded to the European Communities in 1986, represents a huge potential market. The Spaniards smoke three times more cigars than the rest of Europe put together. From personal experience I can inform you that they are smoking most of them in the bar of the European Parliament, and murky simooms hang as hispanic hallmarks over caucuses of conspiring *Allianza Popular*: a right-wing Spanish coalition neither terribly allied, nor indeed desperately popular.

Robert is trying to destroy the myth of Cuban cigar superiority. Havana cigars are no longer what they were, and Royal Jamaica has won three gold medals at the world competition in Brussels for producing the 'finest handmade cigars in the world'. Royal Jamaica is also contemplating avenues of cricket sponsorship in order to promote their image in England. Robert is thinking along the lines of a Royal Jamaica trophy for the batsman scoring the highest number of sixes in the season. Last year the two contenders were Viv Richards and Ian Botham, underpinning the links of sportsmanship and amity between England and the West Indies, and also the contribution of West Indian players to English cricket.

We spent about five hours in the factory, a truly heady experience, with the pungent aroma of fermenting and drying tobacco leaves permeating every corner. Phil was stopped at every tobacco-drugged step to exhibit his Patrick Patterson bruises which had come up a glorious, blue, black, red, and yucky yellow colour.

His performance was exacting the degree of awe-struck respect due to a man who had scored a century. I was reminded forcefully of the gruesome Spanish fascination for the desiccated relics of long-demised saints: bits of arm from Santa Teresa de Avila, bits of finger, bits of toe. Apotheosized overnight to the pantheon of gutsy cricketing heroes, along with the indomitable Brian Close, old Edmonds was religiously unveiling his bits of bruise for the suitably pious cigar-makers to contemplate. They touched it gently, as pilgrims touch the big toe of the bronze statue of St Peter in Rome, and went away to tell the tale. I am afraid it is all going straight to his head. He is now complaining of pains in his hands and feet. A case of incipient stigmata perhaps?

I was getting pretty tired of contemplating Edmonds' dappled and heaving torso, and turned my attention to the women rolling the cigars by hand. From a bundle of tobacco leaves, they are taught to select by feel the three different types of leaf which comprise a cigar. Each cigar is composed of three parts: the Filler, Binder and Wrapper. It was fascinating watching these skilled artisans at their work, feeling, selecting, packing and rolling the leaves into the final impeccable product.

We were sadly obliged to leave the factory at lunchtime, since the team was leaving for Trinidad at two o'clock that afternoon. Robert presented Phil with the most beautiful humedor, made 'in situ', and inlaid with six different hardwoods, including Blue Mahoe, Jamaica's National Wood, and Sandalwood. It was full of personalized Park Lane sized cigars, the wrapper of each bearing the name of Phil Edmonds: an overwhelmingly handsome and generous gift. Phil, unfortunately, has taken to smoking them in bed. I have asked Bob Willis for a different room-mate.

The lobby of the Pegasus was buzzing, as the Press and the team congregated together ready to leave. Unsubstantiated rumours were being tossed around and embroidered upon. Two English journalists, we heard, had been unceremoniously thrown in the slammer on arrival in Trinidad: Geoffrey Boycott (Yorkshire, England and *The Mail on Sunday*) and Matthew Engel, ('Islington Occasionals' and *The Guardian*). Authorities in Port of Spain had no doubt heard what a controversial trouble-maker that Engel is.

8

And so to Trinidad

The flight from Kingston was fairly to moderately dreadful.
The team was listless and apprehensive. The exaggerated,
yet nevertheless disquieting rumours of 5,000 angry Anti-
apartheid protestors rampaging through the streets of Port
of Spain were not designed to imbue us with eager antici-
pation at the thought of our welcome. The press too were
worried about stories of house-arrest, deportation, and work
permits. The team slept sporadically, read half-heartedly
and listened to their 'walkpersons' with the kind of passive
docility vaguely redolent of cows chewing cud. The irrepressible 'Beefy' Botham, however, and the hyper-active
Allan Lamb had a far better idea — until the air hostess pre-
vented them from drinking it.

Ten hours, four stops, three inedible snackettes, and two
bomb scares later we arrive at Piarco Airport, Port of Spain.

'Good morning,' said a bright young man, sporting an
M.C.C. 'Egg and Bacon' tie. 'I'm John Dewdney-Herbert,
British High Commission.' He was, at that hour, a very
friendly and reassuring sight. We were whisked away
immediately, amid tight security, in a rather tinny bus.

'Rebs near the windows,' insisted Phil, though it was
remarked that he had shoved me rather close to one.

We met with absolutely no aggression. Given the ugly
mood of some of the players after ten hours semi-voluntary
aero-incarceration, the Trinidadian protestors were certainly well advised to stay out of our way. Five thousand
raging protestors or not, my money at 2 am that morning
would have been squarely on the England team.

'Not even one fucking brick,' complained one I. T.

Botham, feeling not a little cheated. 'Not even one,' he kept on repeating monotonously again and again and again. The air hostess had patently not managed to stop him having quite a few good ideas, and he ranted on in his own boisterous yet ultimately good-natured fashion.

We arrived at the Trinidad Hilton to a barrage of camera crews, the flashing brilliance of the lights inversely proportional to that of the questions. The long-suffering British TV licence-holder may well feel that a few minutes news coverage justifies the inordinate expenditure lavished on these characters, and yet one cannot help but feel that it might be so much more worthwhile if they got the odd result right. England's amazing victory over the West Indies in the second One-day International was reported on the BBC's *Nine O'clock News* as a defeat. Only the one run in it, admittedly, but a minor detail worth getting straight. The ITN crew, who apparently did a magnificent job in understanding that England had actually won, were subsequently told to burn their Amex cards (and enjoy themselves for the rest of the tour). To a cynical outsider it all seems such a lot for such a little.

Neither TV crew, fortunately, followed us into the lift. We were all tired enough to drop. 'Beefy' was also emotional enough to drop into Les Taylor's arms, and bestow a large smacker of a kiss on his cheek.

An elderly American gentleman looked at me quizzically. 'So this,' he enquired in horrified disbelief, '*this* is the England cricket team?'

The security arrangements for the team are very impressive. We have a team of armed policemen on 24-hour guard outside in the corridor. It takes a bit of getting used to, having a Smith and Wesson riding shot-gun on the early morning tea, but there are some definite advantages to the arrangement. A German woman who has been put on the same corridor as us (I cannot imagine why this should be inflicted on any normal resident, unless she particularly enjoys this Stalag existence), has told me what wonderful baby-sitters these security guards make.

'Darlink, zey are wunderbar. If zee baby cry ven I am out, zey go into zee room, and zey nurse zee baby back to sleep.'

It seemed gratuitous to tell her the truth, and that if certain members of the England touring team (especially P.H.E.) got to her perennially yarling offspring before the policemen, it might well end up in the magi-mix of the Hilton's La Boucan cocktail bar.

The Trinidad Hilton takes some getting used to. Locally it is referred to as the 'Upside Down Hotel', since the lobby is on the ground floor, and the bedrooms, having been constructed on the side of a hill, are in a staggered formation underneath. The architect was obviously a man of some vision and not a little sense of humour. People spend hours huddled together in the lift, in close physical proximity and warm social affability, wondering where the hell to get out.

It is a glorious hotel, set in 25 acres of luxuriant tropical grounds, with all-weather tennis courts; an ingenious swimming pool, carved out in the shape of Trinidad; two good, if devastatingly exorbitant restaurants; a view from our balcony of the Queen's Park Savannah; and the glistening blue harbour beyond.

The claustrophobia of this laager-formation existence, however, is starting to tell on all of us, and yet the team, at least, have one another. I am missing intelligent female company, and feel the lack of it like a physical pain. For a woman used to working and wandering autonomously around the world on her own, it is difficult suddenly to find yourself in somebody else's ball-game, and forbidden to call any of the shots.

Phil never ceases to remind me that I am here on sufferance, and therefore have absolutely no rights whatsoever. If he wants to watch the television or listen to the radio all night I must shut up, and it's *his* tour. Since I too am trying to work, and am paying all the hotel bills, I am beginning to find this attitude not a trifle outrageous. Men on tour are different animals, however; not terribly rational, nor on occasions overwhelmingly pleasant propositions. Not for the first time I have been seriously wondering what benefits there are in being married to a professional cricketer. More than anything, I am beginning to resent being consigned to silence. Phil has ordered me to stop bursting in with my threepence worth on the noble art of cricket, in such egregious company. 'You,' he keeps reminding me forcibly, 'know nothing about it.'

Judging from England's performance in the first two tests, however, it would not seem that I am occupying that spot in glorious isolation, and therefore fail to see why I should be the only one positively disqualified from discussing it. Indeed, the problem with this peripatetic cricketing circus is that so few of them seem desirous or capable of discussing anything else, and if one does not wish to end the tour with vestigial vocal cords, then there is an inevitability of joining in. Besides, I am not entirely convinced that this is the sort of Renaissance forum where the conversation can successfully be turned around to Rabelais' contribution to 16th century French literature, or the ramifications of the Spanish attitude towards NATO. Yes, Man you've got it. I am beginning to feel bored, stultified, restricted and homesick.

Have you ever noticed that when you reach those emotional troughs something always happens to pull you out of it? The phone then rang, a long-distance call from (gosh, dare we mention it?) Johannesburg. It is my friend and fellow conference interpreter, Tineke de Boer, on a three-week holiday in South Africa. Tineke is tall, blonde, attractive, Dutch, an ex-Olympic swimmer, educated in Geneva, speaks seven languages, and possesses nothing which does not issue from a designer boutique.

Honestly, I genuinely do ask myself why I am wandering around the Caribbean in solitary confinement, made to feel awkward and emarginalized by a combination of resentful, suspicious, unsympathetic, guilty-conscience-ridden, socially inadequate, educational sub-to-more-or-less-normal cricketers, when I could be having a riot with the Tinekes of life.

'What is it like in Trinidad?' she asked.

'Drizzling, unfriendly and expensive,' I replied. 'And how about Joey's,' I enquired, with a degree of wistful nostalgia, for friends, opportunities and *temps perdu*.

'Very cheap, very friendly, and brilliant weather,' her voice bounced back enthusiastically off some far-flung satellite. 'Are you enjoying yourself?' she continued.

'Not since we got to Trinidad,' I whined self-pityingly, like some menopausal, Valium-hooked housewife to her long-suffering G.P.

'Only one solution. Go out and spend a lot of money,' suggested Tineke, who has studied economics and household management at the same school as I.

'I'm afraid to,' I whinged, 'after the bollocking Phil gave me for bringing four suitcases, and for my pre-tour excesses at Harrod's. He has told me rather belligerently it was time I save some money.'

'Ma chère,' responded Tineke, unhindered by such minor parasites as husbands and truly horrified at such parsi-monious-niggardly attitudes.

'Ma chère, on ne fait pas des économies, on les hérite. (Darling, you don't make savings, you inherit other people's.)

I suddenly felt quite irrationally happy to be confirmed in my own better judgment: When in doubt, spend. Besides, when all was said and done, I had good reason to go shopping. My dramatically different, super-specific, brilliantly-bionic, exorbitantly-expensive, cellular-renewal, sub-skin, watch-it-girl-you're-over-30 cream had not survived the trip to Trinidad.

Leaving the Hilton, however, was easier said than done. Tony Brown had advised us not to leave the hotel without an armed police escort. Phil, present at the genesis of my shopping trip, suggested that the policeman might usefully hand-cuff me to himself as well. The world, you understand — at least according to Phil — is divided into two categories: the shoppers and the non-shoppers; the builders and the consumers; the spenders and the savers. I am an inveterate and tireless consumer. Phil on the contrary gets that same old psychosomatic pain in the wallet every time he gets within a two-mile radius of New Bond Street. He thinks it is one of the seven deadly sins, for example, to spend money on clothes. Unfortunately not everyone is in the professional sportsman's felicitous and privileged position. Phil gets all his clothes as a series of 'Gimmies' from Austin Reed, Burton's and Grey Nicholl's and the need actually to purchase anything is therefore extremely remote.

He would have happily spent the entire tour in a borrowed pair of Peter Willey's swimming trunks if I had not drawn the line. Grudgingly he purchased two pairs of bathers; a white pair with a florid floral insert and a 38-inch waist, and a diarrhoea-brown pair, of equally generous girth and proportionately little sartorial appeal.

'Oh, God,' groaned Les Taylor, whose aesthetic receptibilities are as deeply refined as my own. 'Hawaii 5-O,' he winced as he saw the white ones. 'It's what we keep our King Edwards in,' he wept as he saw the brown ones. Certainly no one can accuse Phil of anything even vaguely germaine to narcissism.

My shopping trip down town was not entirely crowned with success. There is as much chance of locating Erno Laszlo cosmetics in Port of Spain as of locating a clear tactical strategy in an England team meeting. My police-guard was an extremely affable Indian man, and the conversation turned naturally enough to the cricket. Without prompting he informed me that he, and indeed many members of the Indian community, would not only defy the Prime Minister's injunctions to boycott the cricket, but would actually turn up to support the England team.

'Totally useless and lazy, these blacks,' he erupted suddenly, the outpourings of a chronic, pernicious, racial carbuncle. 'Totally useless. We Indians have all the money. We do all the work. And we run all the business. We run all the farms. The blacks are totally useless, I can tell you!'

'Come off it,' I cajoled him in a tone of bantering disbelief. 'Surely there are a few good ones knocking around?'

'Well,' he compromised grudgingly, 'about one in three thousand.'

It was a statistic as revealing as it was dogmatic. More than anything it demonstrated the internecine racial tensions which permeate and underpin Trinidadian society.

The population on the island is sharply divided: 40 per cent black negroes, 40 per cent Asians, mainly Indians, and a mix of Chinese, European and Middle Eastern accounting for the balance. It is easy to sublimate racial problems when everyone is rolling in the old filthy lucre and laughing all the way to the bank in the brand-new, petrol-guzzling, Trinidadian-assembled, Japanese estate car. As an oil-based economy, Trinidad was coining the boodle in the 1970s while many industrialized nations were reeling from the shock of mammoth OPEC price hikes. Today, the island has been hard hit by the recent slump in world oil prices.

'US$12.70 a barrel on the spot-market,' a Texan oil magnate told me as we watched the flaming sunset dissolve into the pitch-black Port of Spain harbour. The boys were locked in yet another cosmically important team meeting, discussing the finer tactical niceties of what to do on the rest day.

'Yes, Ma'am, US$12.70 a barrel. Which is a mite cheaper than this mighty fine Hilton cocktail it is my pleasure to offer you ma'am.'

It would *have* to be that evening that the usually pitilessly protracted team meeting petered out in ten minutes.

Trinidad's petro-dollars obviated the need for a balanced economy. Too late in the financial day, the government is trying to rationalize a sinfully antediluvian sugar industry, but Luddite attitudes towards mechanical harvesters demonstrated by the Sugar Workers Union are not helping. Diversification has become the new buzz word. The government is experimenting with rice, citrus fruits, coffee and dairy farming, and efforts are being made to reverse the 1970s trend of rural exodus. It is all, however, too little and too late. The Trinidadian dollar had already been devalued by 50 per cent before Christmas 1985. Now, rumours of further devaluation are rife. Inflation is reaching double figures, unemployment is on the increase, and wages are being squeezed. The pecuniary paper which superficially covered the racial cracks is beginning to give: to paraphrase Tom Lehrer, 'The black folks are startin' to hate the Indian folks; an' the Indian folks are startin' to hate the black folks; an' everyone is startin' to hate the Prime Minister' — The People's National Movement (P.N.M.) leader, George Chambers.

It is into this seething, frothing, highly inflammable melting pot that the England cricket team has arrived. It is election year, and for the first time in 30 years it looks as if the P.N.M.'s stifling grip on the country might be broken. The four disparate and fragmented opposition parties have joined forces to form the National Alliance for Reconstruction, and they hope to break the monopoly of the P.N.M., a party shored up mainly by the Black vote.

After months of sitting on the rather shaky and ambiguous fence of political expediency, and after allowing the West Indian Board of Control to stage two Test Matches in Trinidad, Mr Chambers made some electoral capital out of the event. In order to mollify the highly vocal Anti-Apartheid lobby, and to win back the disenchanted Black vote (many of them disillusioned by 30 years of P.N.M. rule, and such a rapid down-turn in the economy), the Prime Minister ostentatiously and officially stated that he personally would be boycotting the cricket. The President, Ellis Clarke, and the External Affairs Minister, Errol Mahabir, immediately followed suit. The ensuing fuss is highly indicative of the significance of the game in the West Indies, and reminds me forcibly of my conversation with that wise old man of Tunapuna, Trinidad, and Brixton, C.L.R. James.

'Cricket,' I remember him say, 'is the only unifying factor

in the West Indies . . . cricket is the only thing that binds them all together.' Was the West Indian love of the game going to prevail over the machinations of power politics?

The next few days would tell, but for a normal, rational human being — a category to which I occasionally belong — it was revealing to contemplate the controversy and political debate which the mere refusal of a West Indian Prime Minister to attend a Test Match could create. Nine out of ten letters to the daily newspapers focused on the phenomenon. It would be difficult to imagine the English Test and County Cricket Board getting its collegiate jock-strap in a twist over Margaret Thatcher refusing to turn up to a Test Match at Lord's. Perhaps Mrs Thatcher would feel, however, along with a lot of other serious and high-minded folk such as myself and the International Monetary Fund, that a Prime Minister's job is to sit at home and sort out a dicey economy, rather than idle five days away watching a cricket match at the Queen's Park Oval.

Well, Mr Chambers has told us he will be sitting at home. The tenth letter to the daily newspapers is suggesting, nevertheless, that he will be watching the cricket on the television. Television! There's a point. The affluent Trinis all have the dreaded box, and their strategically placed satellite dishes pick up signals from a plethora of pirated American TV channels. This, in part at least, explains the wave of Anti-Apartheid demonstrations, a phenomenon barely remarked in Trinidad on the 1981 tour.

Trinidadians have been horrified recently by the American news coverage of the bloody riots, the police beatings and the general oppression of the black community in South Africa. The visual image is inevitably so much more emotive, immediate, and provocative than the written word, and many black negro West Indians have decided that tacit sympathy with their suffering brothers is no longer enough. Whether targeting their pent-up anger and revulsion over the Pretoria regime on the England rebels is right or wrong is irrelevant. It is simply inexorable, and international sportsmen would do well to understand it.

Certainly, exacerbating an already incendiary situation with his comments did not help Graham Gooch's case in the eyes of most of the West Indian, Anti-apartheid faction, and his subsequent complaints about being the focus of the protestors' attention exhibited a genuine naiveté which is highly dangerous in such a complicated world. Go to South Africa, by all means. Take the loot. But let's muster the imagination to realize that some people are bound to object.

9

Engel makes his mark

The Second One-day International was, according to people who know about these things, 'the most exciting game of cricket ever'. People who know about these things make sure they never get the time to know about anything else by endlessly reminiscing about all these multifarious 'most exciting games of cricket ever'. It is a repetitive process which gradually anaesthetizes the brain into amnesing all those even more multifarious 'most terribly turgid games of cricket ever', a useful phenomenon which ensures that the noble art of cricket can stagger on supported.

Anyway, this was definitely another 'most exciting game of cricket ever'. A brilliant knock by Viv Richards (82 runs off 39 balls) seemed to have guaranteed another West Indian victory. Protestors outside hearing the excited and enthusiastic cheers were seen to drop their placards in an indecent 'bugger the demo, we want to see the master' hurry to purchase late entry tickets. The Queen's Park Oval, despite official boycotts and P.N.M. threats of reprisal on any government employee seen lurking there, was filled to capacity. The West Indian love of cricket had once again superseded petty politics and pusillanimous politicians.

Aspects of Black Power were also festering not far from the surface. People turned up to see the cricket, yes, but some came to see a white humiliation, to see 'West Indies . . . grind England to the dust', as the eponymous Eddy Odingi put it so charmingly in the 10th March edition of the *Trinidad Express*. 'Grinding folk to dust', in our social, democratic and we're-all-so-terribly-liberal days is the sort of nauseating vocabulary common only to extremes of white and black. All extremes end up preaching the same lessons of physical oppression and colour hatred. Sport may well succeed in breaking down barriers. The tragedy is that there are always the partisan supporters, the black-and-white viewers of life to build them all up again.

The most glorious of ironies inevitably happened; Graham Gooch, the villain of the Trinidadian piece, made 129 brilliant runs to become their overnight darling. Superlatives fail for his magnificent, virtually single-handed achievement: *his* victory. No one individual could have done more to restore England's pride, and pull the team from its slough of 'can't face the fast bowlers' despond, to the pinnacles of gung-ho 'in-and-at-them' optimism.

While the English popular press hastily turned the pages of the communal Roget's Thesaurus from synonyms for excruciatingly execrable to synonyms for exquisitely exhilarating exhibition — pages A to D and F to Z were lost on the 1981 trip, which explains the paucity of vocabulary in certain tabloids — Viv Richards, apparently in some cosmic Caribbean sulk, was refusing to give interviews.

All this was in sharp contrast, however, to the way in which two of my dearest colleagues, Geoffrey Boycott and Matthew Engel, were welcomed to this lovely island.

Geoff left Kingston the day before the team, and Matthew 'I-too-can-be-a-sleuth-especially-when-there-is-no-cricket-to-write-about' Engel decided there might be a story in Geoff's reception at Piarco Airport, Trinidad. Geoff's South African connections had been causing much controversy, and politicians, trade union leaders, customs and immigration officials, waiters, porters, and upstairs maids had all threatened to give him a hard time, though I do have it on excellent authority from a highly placed diplomatic source that not a single one of them was in the pay of the Yorkshire C.C.C.

Sure enough, Geoff was stopped by an immigration official, who looked at his passport and made an immediate phone-call. 'Ah-ha,' thought Matthew, taking copious mental notes, 'this is an interesting development.'

Two mintues later, Matthew still taking copious notes was himself an integral part of the same interesting development, as the Ministry of National Security decided to deport the pair of them. The spurious reason given for this disgracefully cavalier treatment of Yorkshire's finest bat and England's 'Sportswriter of the Year' was the fact that they had no work permits. Journalists and cricket correspondents visiting Trinidad for short periods, covering specific occasions, have never before needed permits, and the authorities' attitude to English press men was dolefully reminiscent of the most counter-productive excesses of the Pretoria government itself.

But for an accident of time-table scheduling, and the fact that there was no plane back to England that night, the Ministry of National Security would have sent Geoff and Matthew home, deported unceremoniously as illegal immigrants and undesirable aliens. Had Geoff and Matthew not taken the forward flak and alerted the British authorities to the situation, a similar fate would have attended the entire English press corps the next day and the Ministry would have had them all deported, lock, stock and venomous 'tripewriter'. I have been given unequivocally to understand, however, that there is absolutely no truth in the rumours that anyone in the Ministry is in the pay of either Ian Botham or Bob Willis, and it is comforting to ascertain that paranoid dislike and neurotic suspicion of the press is not confined merely to cricketing circles.

Rumours abounded, the more unsubstantiated the better, amongst the departing press corps in Kingston. First, we learned that Geoff and Matthew actually *had* been deported. Then we heard that they had been thrown in the slammer. They had, in fact, been placed under house arrest in the Holiday Inn, which although it has gone down in the past few years, is still not really as bad as all that. Matthew was staggered to find that the phone had not been cut off and he had not been left totally incommunicado. Could he phone his copy, he asked the telephonist, through to *The Guardian*? It really was important. The telephonist, as it happened, was an Indian lady.

'I think it is a scandal, the way they are treating you,' she opined sympathetically, and gave his call top priority treatment.

Meanwhile, back in Kingston, there was no shortage of suggestions for Matthew's headline; 'My night of torment and terror in the slammer with Geoffrey' seemed to be gathering support as a 'goodie' from the popular press corps. Matthew was just the slightest bit peeved two days later when Peter Smith of the *Mail* appeared to know more about the entire incident than Matthew himself. Quite a revelation for a journalist, no doubt, to be on the wrong end of a news story for once!

The British High Commissioner, Sir Martin Berthoud, was immediately informed of the two men's arrest, and diplomatic telexes between London and Port of Spain were whizzing back and forth all night, as Geoff and Matthew slept soundly under the watchful eyes of personalized armed guards. It seemed a bit like a Trinidadian hammer to crack an Islington walnut: Matthew is not built in the palaeolithic Edmonds—Botham mould, and is as likely to confront a police-guard, armed or otherwise, as Graham Gooch is to indulge in social niceties with me.

'The night of torment and terror' was mercifully short-lived. Sir Geoffrey himself (Howe not Boycott) asked to be kept personally informed of developments, and the High Commissioner was told to lodge the strongest possible protest with the Trinidadian authorities, which in diplomatic parlance would probably read something like this:

'Dear Trinidadian Authorities,
We think this is a jolly poor show.
    Yours ever,
    British High Commissioner.

P.S. Sir Geoffrey is awfully cross too.
P.P.S. Thanks for an absolutely wonderful
    cocktail party last Tuesday.'

It is just this kind of Palmerstonian 'send-in-the-gun-boats-and-bugger-up-the-cocktail-party' talk that made the British Empire great, and made the British Imperial Army what it was: a bunch of party-wrecking-fight-pickers.

The Trinidadian authorities were obviously shaken to the deepest profundities of their reverberating maracas, and quivered under the full force of British opprobrium. The fact that the entire Trinidadian Press Corps threw an absolutely major wobbly (concerned, quite rightly, about the freedom of the press in general, and retaliatory measures against themselves in particular), was probably not entirely irrelevant either, and the Trinidadian Government was obliged to make a major climb-down in this monumental cock-up. The Empire struck back and Boycott and Engel were Free Men.

The government, of course, had to save face, and therefore insisted that since they could not deport the members of the press, they would at least charge them £120 each for the privilege of working. £120 to work for a fortnight! It's the kind of wheeze the Tories could contemplate to improve the economy!

Peter Smith, who looks after the press corps' material needs and co-ordinates travel arrangements in a gently patriarchal sort of way, showed me the list of English journalists for whom work permits had finally been granted. The Ministry of National Security had placed a black mark by the name of any journalist who had been to South Africa. The fact that many, if not most, of the people concerned had been filing exactly the sort of copy that is undermining the Pretoria regime, and is making people (including West Indians) all over the world react to the system of apartheid, was patently of no relevance to these bureaucratic, bi-neurone minds. Tarring journalists who had put their personal safety on the line to write vehemently anti-apartheid pieces with the same mindless brush as the 'I only wanted to play cricket and the money was good' brigade, seemed to me a fundamentally despicable and unforgivable injustice.

The British High Commissioner was delighted that the situation had been so neatly and successfully defused. He knows, unlike the Trinis, that we do not have that many gunboats left. No one in the Foreign and Commonwealth office, not even in the wildest allowable diplomatic hyperbole, would describe Trinidad as a hive of mega-politic activity, and the Boycott—Engel episode had created quite a stir.

'It's all been so exciting,' Sir Martin Berthoud confided to me at his cocktail party. 'I've only been here 18 months and so much has happened. First George Chambers went to England. Then the Queen came here. And now *this*. I've been on the front of all the English Dailies, photographs of me and Michael Boycott.'

'Geoffrey,' corrected Phil gently.

'Quite so, John,' Sir Martin smiled at Phil, 'Geoffrey.'

As one who has always felt that games should end with puberty, I was pleased to ascertain that 'Our Man in Port of Spain' had placed cricket and cricketers in their proper perspective, as significant 'per se' as Jenkin's ear, but capable of causing just as much aggro. Geoffrey was at the party, and looking as impeccably smart as always. Many people accuse Geoff of being selfish and self-centred, and a player who could remain nameless but who is sometimes known as Neil Foster, took the trouble to underline every, 'I', 'myself' and 'me' in Geoff's *Mail on Sunday* account of the affair. Admittedly, there were quite a few, and Matthew was much miffed that Geoff had not mentioned him even half as much as he had mentioned Geoff. I find Geoff great fun, however, and his conversation certainly holds no trace of those self-pitying recriminations that seem to inform other anti-apartheid targets' every utterance.

'They had to let me go, Frances,' he laughed. 'Too hot to handle.'

'I'd rather have a jokey egotist than a surly whinger any day.

Dear Matthew, however, is now suffering from a bad dose of Fame, and is taking the mickey out of himself unmercifully.

'Can't write today,' he announced in a world-weary, mega-star sort of way. 'Lost my black, medium gauge BIC ballpoint.'

Judging by the seven o'clock shadow he now seems to be affecting, he must have mislaid his disposable BIC razor as well. Despite all efforts, however, he looks no more like an ex-con than . . . than . . . well, it is difficult off-hand, but there are one or two of the press corps who could finish my simile neatly.

To everyone's surprise, and to the 'we're sick of touring and want to go home' lobby's disappointment, the actual demonstrations were rather an anodyne chapter after such a fulminating exordium. One almost felt tempted to feel that the Trinis were in a post-carnival depression, and basically just needed something to make a song and dance about.

'They've got some really catchy little tunes,' Phil remarked, impressed. In fact, they're so catchy we've got Allan Lamb joining in.

'Taylor, Thomas, Go Home,' he keeps singing at the top of his voice, his clipped South African accent reverberating gaily from the hollow depths of the shower room.

The irony of the situation is not lost on 'Legga'. (Legga Lamb. Get it? The team's inventive genius, not mine.) He is the only South African in the England team, and it has for-tunately not occurred to even the most rabid of protestors to complain about him. He is growing constantly in everyone's esteem on this tour. His indefatigable determination in the practice nets, his stalwart and gutsy performances in the middle, and his perennially cheerful good humour are shin-ing examples to some of the moaners.

I have only ever heard him complain once this tour, and

1 The England team before setting out: *back row* Robinson, Smith, Taylor, Thomas, Edmonds, Ellison, Foster, Downton and French. *front row* Gooch, Botham, Gatting, Gower, Lamb, Willey and Emburey.

2 At the outset, there was considerable optimism that if the England batsmen could contain the West Indian coterie of fast bowlers there was an even chance that they could share the series. However, from the outset, England was faced with bowling of such speed that they seldom made any headway. Bouncers became the order of the day from both sets of bowlers.

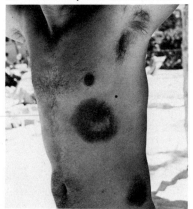

(a) Phil's body after being hit by balls from Patterson, despite having worn a protective corset.
(b) *above right:* Gower fends off Patrick Patterson.
(c) *below:* Gooch loses his helmet.

(d) *above:* Greenidge on the receiving end of a ball from Greg Thomas.
(e) *below:* Malcolm Marshall caught Mike Gatting a nasty blow
in the face, breaking his nose. The England vice-captain
had to return home to London for repairs.

3 The pre-tour hype suggested there would be large anti-apartheid rallies. While the team was confronted with some opposition because of the inclusion of the South African 'Rebels' – Gooch, Taylor, Emburey and Willey – in the England side, it received far more publicity than it deserved. Island politicians jumped on the bandwagon and, as a result, the England team was closely guarded, particularly in Trinidad.

(a) A policeman belted up with all manner of goodies.
(b) An apartheid poster in Antigua.

4 Ian Botham became the central figure both on and off the field as the tabloids did their best to undermine his very being. *The Guardian* ranked him second only to the Royal Family, Eastenders and Dallas as a public property.

(a) Padded up for practice.
(b) In a pensive moment.
(c) Relaxing, with David Gower.

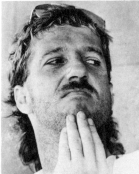

5 Viv Richards, successor to Clive Lloyd as captain of the West Indies, got on with his job.

6 Viv's parents, Malcolm and Gratel Richards, with their grand-daughter, Matara.

7 Meetings were the order of the day:

(a) The Press quiz Tony Brown (manager) and David Gower.
Note my favourite journalist, Matthew Engel (Mount Gay and
The Guardian, second right), shields Scyld Berry (the *Observer*).
(b) At Lemon Arbour, I instigated an alternative meeting
for the non-cricketers.

NOT THE ENGLAND TEAM ROOM.

NORMAL OPENING HOURS

TACTICS + STRATEGIES STRICTLY
                        PROHIBITED.

NOT THE NEXT TEAM MEETINGS:
a) 18/4/86 } TOPIC: (SAME AS TEAM MEETING)
b) 20/4/86 } "WHAT TO DO ON REST DAY".

8 The author, at play.

that was the morning after I apparently forced him to drink an entire bottle of Phil's Hine Vieille Fine Champagne antique cognac. It was during that evening that he told me he was walking around the island the next day for the benefit of leukaemia research. I had done sufficiently well out of Phil's second bottle of Hine Vieille Fine Champagne antique cognac to sponsor him for five dollars a mile, and was not a trifle confused the next day when I heard on the radio that one A. Lamb was fielding at slip . . .

10

The media circus

The first day of the Second Test proved that Viv Richards would be wasting his time bothering to learn any 'winning isn't everything' speeches. England's innings was a depressingly *déjà-vu* performance.

With the exception of Gower and lynch-pin Lamb, the batting looked as shaky as a good dose of *delerium tremens*, and the score did not even reach 200. The trouble with this sort of performance is that it inexorably leads to even greater mediocrity. Specialist bowlers are sacrificed in ever more frenzied attempts to shorten a tail which resolutely refuses to wag. It can get bloody frustrating if you're a specialist bowler, and bowling rather well. My husband is a specialist bowler. And he is bowling rather well. It remains to be seen what happens as the tour develops.

The second day of the Second Test was Phil's thirty-fifth birthday. He arrived back at the hotel after bowling virtually all day in insufferably hot and humid conditions. He undid his surgical corset and flung himself on the bed, hardly able to move. I felt like 'Mrs Rocky II'.

My idea of a quiet, romantic, candle-lit birthday dinner flew out of our seventh floor Hilton window, as Phil's sullen, cold-eyed, filthy bad temper became more and more apparent. Was it the fact that someone had missed a stumping, and someone else had missed a catch? Was it (oh, unspeakable bitch that I am) because the off-spinner, John Emburey, had picked up five wickets and Phil only two? Was it something far less serious: a sudden attack of mid-life-crisis-male-menopause-precipitated-by-35th-birthday syndrome? Mild dyspepsia? A tiny cardiac arrest? Rampant jock-rot?

Simon Barnes of *The Times* pitched up to talk to Phil about their book: *Phil Edmonds: A Singular Man*. It is still not too late to change the title to *Phil Edmonds: A Single Man*.

Phil took Simon out to dinner. I went to bed. It is high time, I felt, that Phil gave up this game. He is getting far too old and far too cantankerous. At 35 it is time he acceded to committee status. Failing that, I shall have to have a word with that dear boy, Patrick.

We met Patrick Patterson at the British High Commissioner's cocktail party, given in honour of the two teams.

'So you're the guy who nearly killed my husband,' I said, failing miserably to strike fear and trembling into his juvenile, Jamaican heart.

He smiled an engagingly shy and winsome smile, his two small, ever-so-slightly-protruding ears sticking out from the side of his head like the handles on a black *Le Creuset* soup tureen.

'Better luck next time,' I encouraged him in my disarmingly engaging Lucretia Borgia way. 'There could be a few bob in it for you.'

I never cease to be amazed at the kind, gentle, almost docile nature of the most viciously hostile fast bowlers off the field. Their natural male aggression is presumably all spent in the act of bowling, and all that is left is sweetness and light. If they played cricket in Europe, I'm sure some Teutonic Doctor-Doctor Professor-Professor would by now have evolved some cricket-based therapy theory: 30 overs of bouncers against the photograph of your hate-fixation. It would save a lot of real estate devoted to rooms with soft walls, and would give the sagging European truss industry just the lift it needs.

Our new English fast hope, Greg 'Blodwen' Thomas who is of course a Welshman, is the most charmingly affable person you could ever wish to meet. Sporting his rimless spectacles, he looks more likely to tune your fiddle at an eisteddfod than separate your head from your shoulders with a quick delivery. The myth of tough macho quickies was definitively exploded for me when I learned that Australian Jeff 'Thommo' Thompson grew orchids for a hobby.

It was a myth which had already begun to disintegrate when Phil and I looked after an influenza-ridden Middlesex, West Indian pace-man, Wayne Daniel. Poor Wayne had left his sunny Barbadian paradise, lured with tales of lovely Lord's and St John's Wood streets paved with gold, to do his registration for Middlesex. Pre-season training in the usual Arctic conditions had left Wayne suffering from a bad attack of rhetorical questions like 'What the hell am I doing here?', and a nasty dose of 'flu. Dear old Waynie! His generally cheerful black face was covered in a kind of grey patina, the sort of colour juxtaposition you see on chocolates that have lain too long in the fridge, or are in the process of going off.

I gave him a plaque-stripping concoction of Glenfiddich, Lemsip, paracetamol, honey and cloves, and we put him to bed with a hot water bottle (an unfamiliar rubbery item of which Wayne was understandably suspicious), in the spare room of our newly-marrieds' Chelsea love-nest. It was not entirely felicitous that my younger brother Brendan (yes, our Man in Jamaica), still up at Cambridge, had a key to the establishment: sleeping it off when pissed in town for the use of. Phil and I were awoken by a tremendous racket and turned on the lights in the spare room to discover one petrified, delirious black West Indian; one confused, intoxicated white undergraduate; and one large pink flaccid hot water bottle all doing battle for pre-eminence in a small single bed. Wayne never stayed with us again.

We are hoping to see old Daniel on this tour in Barbados, though he had already threatened Phil that he is 'after' him. Phil and I managed to turn up 24 hours late for Wayne's end of benefit-season dinner-dance. I don't eat and Phil doesn't dance, but for Wayne, who more than anyone in the team has put Middlesex in its dominant county position, we were prepared to make an exception. Sunday night *did* seem rather a strange night to hold the function, but there it was, carefully pencilled into Phil's new 'Filofax' system.

Phil had long envied my Filofax, a three year compilation of names, addresses, telephone numbers, appointments, commitments, birthdays, bank account numbers, restaurants, hotels . . . If I ever lost it, I swear governments will fall. I purchased a similar breviary for Phil in a last-ditch effort to put a bit of order into the Byzantine chaos of his highly under-developed personalized filing system. I cannot imagine that J. Paul Getty or Aristotle Onassis cracked the world's wheeler-dealer financial circuit by keeping the numbers of Swiss bank accounts on the back of other people's Woodbine packets, and it is on the advanced Woodbine packet philosophy that Phil's filing system is precariously predicated. All the necessary information is compiled and collated somewhere. The problem is retrieval.

Phil accepted his gift with puerile joy, and promised faithfully to use it always. The only indispensible adjunct to a successful Filofax, however, is the capacity to fill it in correctly. Phil and I arrived at the Lord's Tavern banqueting suite, at the appointed time, a blaze of black velvet, feathers and silver sequins. (Incidentally, I looked pretty smart as well.) The dinner-dance, Cerberus the gateman at Lord's informed us, had happened — the night before. All dressed up and nowhere to go, we bought a box of Kentucky Fried Chicken from the Holland Park Avenue outlet, and discarding the family fender tucked into it on the way home.

Phil was genuinely upset. But, with our sponsored double ticket at £50, not half as upset as Wayne. He has therefore promised to 'fix' Phil, should their paths cross in Barbados. Poor Wayne. He'll just have to wait his turn.

Life in this hermetically-sealed Trinidad Hilton bubble is starting to pall. The Press back home, so we hear, is devoting many column inches to the unmerciful slating of the team in general, and the beleaguered Ian Botham, in particular. On tour the press lives in inevitably close physical proximity with the rest of us. They eat, drink, live, enjoy themselves and travel with us, and yet, of course, they do have a job to do.

Unfortunately, it is sometimes a job which can be inimical to the criteria of an intimate friendship. Journalists are often obliged to write harsh, objective and fairly *ad hominem* criticism, and some of the mega-egos on tour find even the vaguest hint of opprobrium difficult to stomach. Within certain fairly nebulous parameters, however, a fairly healthy working relationship between the players and the team should be possible, but a degree of anti-press paranoia is sadly beginning to permeate the team.

Bob Willis continues to regard the press with the deepest suspicion, not unnaturally after his own often unsympathetic and even shoddy treatment as captain at their ink-stained hands. Ian Botham is quite understandably furious at some of the character assassination being meted out to him, though his failure thus far to perform with either bat or ball has added grist to the 'Cut Botham down to size' mill.

The team, however, is guilty of one totally comprehensible injustice. They should not fall into the counter-productive trap of tarring all members of the press with the same suspicious brush. The regular cricket correspondents accredited to the tour are, by and large, an extremely decent bunch. Characters like John Woodcock (*The Times*), and Peter Smith (the *Daily Mail*), have spent a professional lifetime forging links of mutual understanding, honour and trust between themselves and successive England Touring Teams. It is tragically unfair that these links are currently being tried to breaking-point, if not definitively sundered, by a different 'genre' of journalist: a roving band of 'shock-horror' cads who have inundated the 'regular' press corps.

The paucity of television coverage on Caribbean tours, compounded with the incontrovertibly sad fact that England losing is far better news than England winning has precipitated this plague of venomous typewriter toting scorpions. They fly out at the drop of a sub-editor's hat to join the motley crew of 'World Exclusive', 'Phew What A Scorcher' artists, and parasite on to the cricket-host. These charlatans are not, of course, in any way interested in the game. Most of them never go to watch a match of cricket. They do not really know the players. They simply stick around in the bar, the disco, or the swimming pool like some burgeoning bacteria, waiting to erupt with the next noxious outpourings of their monosyllabic minds and their pernicious prose, desperate to justify their enormous tabloid expenses with any piece of genuine gilt-edged gutter filth they can dredge up.

There is one journalist, in particular, whose meteoric trajectory into the gutter is firmly anchored to his relationship-breaking tales of royalty and sportsmen. But extra-marital affairs are not public property in my book. The great British public does *not* have the right to know. Wayward husbands and wayward wives are accountable to no one, except perhaps, their better halves and ultimately (what a good old convent concept), their consciences. Fortunately, nowadays, few people suffer from the latter.

It is pointless to pretend that three and four month tours are not going to involve a fair amount of hanky-panky. There are quite a few ships, or even British Airways 747's, that pass in the night. The regular press corps turns a very blind eye to what goes on with any degree of discretion. And so they should. Not every one of them is a paradigm of marital probity either. The problem is, if internationally famous figures are dumb or naive enough to cavort ostentatiously with the latest female acquisition under the full glare of the international press, something is bound to percolate home. It is touchingly surprising how desperately discreet and paternally protective the genuine cricket correspondents are, and the lengths to which they will go to keep the lid on things. It really is a gentleman's club, based on many a tacit gentleman's agreement. The problem with the club on this tour, however, is the unstoppable admission of so many non-members. The pressures of four month tours on a marriage, however, is a problem I have already mentioned. It is just one or two members of the press who have recently got my goat up.

Suffice it to say, that whatever these prurient pens are scribbling, the stories of sex, drugs and drink are wildly exaggerated. I've seen more argey-bargey in three days of plenary week in the Strasbourg Holiday Inn, with certain egregious members of the European Parliament trying desperately to get the odd directly-elected leg over than in three months touring with the entire England cricket team. Who has the right to cast the first stone? Homesick and homeless people are understandably liable to misbehave, and we are all, as the French say, adult and vaccinated. Some of the guys it is true would do well to be more vaccinated than others, and judging from some of the dubious late-night ethnic 'Room Service' wandering around on our corridor, prophylactic penicillin might not be counter-indicated either.

Back to the press! Equally divisive as the filth dredgers is the brigade of peripatetic bright boys, the roving columnists who rock in for a couple of days, gain a few superficial impressions, and rock off to file a pile of inflammatory copy from a very comfortable distance. They rely on being a good six or seven thousand miles away before any of their berated victims gets half a whiff of what has been written.

Unfortunately in Trinidad, the media boomerang returned quicker than expected. The *Trinidad Express* of the 12th March carried extracts, out of context, of pieces filed the previous day to London by Ian Wooldridge, award-winning feature writer of the *Daily Mail*, and by *The Times* freelance, Simon Barnes. The target of both pieces was the luckless Ian Botham. According to the *Trinidad Express*, Ian Wooldridge adverted to Botham's 'disgruntled scowl of a street gang bully' and Simon Barnes described Botham as acting 'like a star with a right to strut and bully and make an utter fool of himself'. All this was bad enough, but far worse was the fact that both columnists made reference to how much happier the team was without Botham in India. Neither of them had actually been with the team in India, and both of them, whilst possibly accurate about the atmosphere in the England dressing-room, and players' boredom with touring, had only been in Trinidad a mere few days. Never mind, off roved Wooldridge, to another trouble-shooting assignment. That was perfectly OK. That is the way he operates.

More serious in terms of fall-out for us was the effect of Simon Barnes' piece. Simon had been flown out to Trinidad, courtesy of the publishers William Heinemann, in order to put the finishing touches to his book with Phil. Rightly or wrongly, he was thus associated in the players' minds with Phil. Wrongly, the views he expressed were taken as reflecting Phil's own views. He had been there no time at all, and he had never been seen on tour before. The all-embracing views he expressed were perceived to have come directly from Phil. The *Trinidad Express* had inadvertently dropped Phil and Simon in it. At the subsequent team meeting Both was absolutely furious with Simon and shouted at Phil. Phil was absolutely furious with Simon and shouted at me. Next time I shall encourage Both to shout at me directly, and cut out all the middlemen.

I certainly am getting tired of being the constant whipping-boy on this tour. Not that I feel for a minute that journalists should be in any way inhibited from writing harshly critical copy. I myself have been known to opine that some of the England team are not exactly Mensa material, and that others often appear totally vacant. Such comments, to my lights, are merely somewhere between brutally realistic, and almost generous. The difference is that I have known many of these cricketers, and their personal and professional development over the best part of ten years. I have been going on Phil's sporadic tours since 1978, and whatever I say at all events in no way queers a regular correspondent's pitch: it just ensures that certain people never talk to me ever again — there is, in my madness, a definite method.

It was fortunate that the Test Match rest-day was before this particular storm in the vacuum-packed Hilton teacup blew up. Zeus, contrary to Homeric misconceptions, is obviously a West Indian. The rest day was filled with torrential downpours. Similar weather the next day would have saved the Test Match for England, and it is beginning to look disturbingly possible that only a miracle or the apocalypse is going to obviate another total 'Blackwash'.

The staff of the British High Commission had organized a trip to the Coroni Swamp bird sanctuary, to see Trinidad's most famous bird, the scarlet ibis. We were following in the reportedly disgruntled wake of H.R.H. The Duke of Edinburgh. He had made a similar trip some six months previously, during the Queen's visit to the Caribbean, but his enthusiasm for wild life in general did not, that day at least, extend to the poor old scarlet ibis. (This incidentally is information from a highly placed and very undiplomatic source.)

It was somewhat unfortunate that I had taken cover in the poolside bar during one of the early morning showers with my publisher, Derek Wyatt. Matching an ex-England Rugby International 'Hilton Swizzle' for 'Hilton Swizzle' (a combination of ad hoc liqueurs) does not go down in history as one of my more inspired ideas. *Un peu trop* as Cocteau so rightly wrote *est juste assez pour moi*. (A bit too much is just about enough for me.)

By the time we arrived at the swamp I was in any event seeing large red flying objects in front of my eyes and it was no easy job to distinguish them from the real thing. The scarlet ibis according to un-Swizzled bird-watchers, is a large red bird. Its colour develops over about three years, and is due to the carotene in the crustaceans on which the bird feeds. Flocks of these gorgeous creatures fly in to nest in the Coroni swamp, and monitors do their best to keep the poachers out. It is distressing that these people's nefarious activities are encouraged by the requirements of the famous Trinidad carnival's feathered 'papageno' costumes.

The next day, the last day of the Test Match, the West Indians crossed the i's, dotted the t's, and underlined the lot.

England simply cannot cope. It was a sad reflection on England's generally poor batting performance that the highlight of the match from the England team's point of view was probably the resolute last-ditch second innings stand between the two tail enders Richard Ellison and Greg Thomas. Ian Botham's current lack of form is giving rise to even more tremendous speculation and criticism in the press. How the British love to build their heroes up then cut them down to size. Radio commentators were talking about the 'Criminal waste' of giving him the new ball, and suggesting that the captain, David Gower, should be using Richard Ellison instead. Neither were observers slow to notice that the captain was apparently loath to contradict Botham in anything he wanted to do . . .

Press — player relations are reaching a fairly low ebb. The management convened a meeting with the press in an effort to establish a *modus vivendi* for the rest of the tour. It was by all accounts a pretty acerbic session, with neither side pulling any punches. The management was concerned about some of the exaggerated and unconstructive criticism being written. The press was aggrieved at the anti-press paranoia being exhibited by a few of the players and by a general lack of helpful direction from the top. Quite a few bitter home truths were aired, and it is presently difficult to tell whether the atmosphere had been improved or further exacerbated.

The management then decided to call yet another team meeting. Phil, for one, was rather staggered to hear Bob Willis remark that this was the worst tour he had ever been on in terms of team spirit. No one, for example, complained the manager, Tony Brown, was using the team room. Poor darling! He ought to have a word with the chamber maid, Rose. 'Dat room sure is one man's brothel,' she moaned to me as she collapsed her 16-stone frame into an easy chair and accepted a cool drink. 'What dat boy gettin' up to, no man's business.' Darling Rose has not yet sold her soul to the *Sunday Mirror*, and sadly no amount of cool drink would persuade her to reveal the identity of 'dat boy'. Tony and the

T.C.C.B., however, would no doubt be pleased that the team room is not going entirely to waste.

Bob then went on to complain that the team was riddled with 'cliques'. A few of the younger players were apparently obliged to stifle somewhat cynical giggles. Willis, Gower, Lamb and Botham are known to many of them as the 'gang of four', and immediately after the team meeting the Gang had a rendezvous with a well-appointed yacht. Nothing 'cliquey', you understand, but there were just not enough appointments for everyone.

The word 'clique' sounds unnecessarily pejorative for a totally comprehensible and even inevitable phenomenon on tour. Sixteen grown men cannot tag around with one another in crocodile formation like a Doctor Barnardo's day outing. Sub-groups are bound to develop. Ian Botham, Bob Willis, David Gower, and Allan Lamb are old hands and have known one another and played with one another for years. It is natural therefore that they tend to stay together. Whether this degree of familiarity between the assistant manager and current players is deleterious to general authority and discipline is one of the recurrent leitmotifs of press criticism, but Bob stalwartly maintains that he is just here to count the cricket balls. I personally am extremely grateful to him for managing to organize my vast array of luggage as well. He grouses a lot less than my own husband.

John Emburey and Graham Gooch, two of the South African Rebels, form another mini-groupette. Commonly they are referred to as 'The Siamese Twins', because they are so totally inseparable. I believe that they are even beginning to sound like one another, though it is difficult to comment on the veracity of that since Graham Gooch has not seen fit to indulge me with a word of his sparkling conversation for the past two months. Phil, ever defensive, puts it down to shyness and admittedly I often encount difficulty in discerning the difference between shy and down-right sullen. The *Mail on Sunday* carried a story that he was simply tired of touring, and did not want to go on the next trip to Australia, a sad loss to the England batting line-up, no doubt, but perhaps a decision that would be better for his personal peace of mind and happiness.

This is the mid-point of the tour, and many other members of the team seem similarly worn and weary. These three and four month tours are an anachronism today. Most men, even the gayest dogs, tire of the meretricious pleasures of touring life after a few weeks, and pine for the lowly domestic comforts of home. Everyone is looking forward to moving on to Barbados. That is to be, as Matthew Engel neatly put it, 'the T.C.C.B.-approved conjugal visit'.

11

Lemon Arbour

The 13th March. Piarco Airport. Earlier in the morning than is consonant with conventional concepts of 'beauty sleep'.

No one, it seemed, was devastated to leave Trinidad. On the contrary, there was a definite spring in most people's steps at the thought of the imminent arrival of the 'loved ones'. Strong men, not normally perceived as 'softies', bore a decidedly less prickly demeanour. Peter Willey was mooning around in the Duty Free, carefully selecting a bottle of Harvey's Bristol Cream for his wife Charmaine. Newly-wed nice boy, Neil Foster, was buying chocolates for his darling, Romany. The 'not good in the morning' faction had their 'Walkpersons' rammed firmly into their anti-social ears. Greg Thomas read stories about himself in *The Cricketer* magazine, and tried hard to believe them. The same old well-worn jokes were doing the rounds:

'What does the acronym N.A.S.A. stand for?' Answer: 'Need Another Seven Astronauts'.

And the current South African joke: 'Why does President Botha refuse to play chess?' Answer: 'Because he doesn't know what to do with his black bishop.'

It is not exactly high-brow stuff, but it passes these endless hours we seem to spend hanging around in airports.

Richard Ellison, Phil and I were busily concocting rather puerile epigrams. Well, Elly and I were busily concocting. Phil, I am beginning to notice, is jolly good at simply repeating. A sample of more repeatable efforts would be:

'My name's Elly,
And you'll agree,

The new ball's for me,
Despite Both's wobbly.'

and

'My name's "Henri" (Phil's nickname)
I report sadly
The team all shun me
'Cos Simon's mon ami.'

Nothing for silver-Latin satirist Juvenal to turn in his mausoleum over, I'm obliged to concede. Lengthier distaff laments soon followed:

'It's cricket, bloody cricket,
It's all they do and think,
It's cricket when you're eating
It's cricket when you drink.
And if you think you'll change them
Sister you're out of luck
'Cos it's cricket, bloody cricket
When you want to have a . . . cup of tea.'

It was on this apogee of cultural and poetic achievement that we were called upon to board the plane.

The England cricket team, the West Indian cricket team, the entire 'pilot fish' press corps, and a few normal travellers were all packed into the same BWIA island-hopper. An hour's delay was inevitable as the flight's cargo of fresh, bound-for-Barbados, prawns had to be off-loaded to accommodate cricket coffins, TV camera crew equipment and my four suitcases. I watched the prawns broiling away on the tarmac, salmonella, botulism and God knows what else making merry under the early morning sun. I made a distinct mental note to avoid all seafood buffets in Barbados.

The West Indian team were seated at the front, and the crew of giddily tittering air hostesses raced around providing them with long, exotic looking drinks, bejewelled with maraschino cherries. Aft, in the ninepennies, the England team was having a hard time trying to extract the odd glass of water. Nobody, so it would seem, loves a loser.

We arrived some 45 minutes later to a rum punch party at Grantley Adams international airport, Barbados, and were whisked away (all too speedily for some) to our next two-week home, the Rockley Resort and Beach Club, to the south-west of the island.

The drive from the airport to the hotel was rather a disappointment: narrow winding roads hugged by weather-beaten, clapboard houses, and dull overcast skies. Not exactly the island paradise I had been anticipating. The hotel, to my initial chagrin, was not on the beach but right in the middle of a golf-course. Our unit is actually situated directly behind the seventh green and as I write an over-pitched ball has bounced through my patio and on to the bed. What the hell! I'll just lob the thing back on to the green, and give the poor blighter an Edmonds-sponsored break.

After about two days here, however, I am beginning to enjoy the set-up thoroughly. The Rockley is a self-catering and time-sharing Resort. The accommodation is arranged in 'clusters', each with its own swimming pool and tropical gardens, and there are central facilities of squash and tennis courts, restaurant, bar, supermarket, shops and disco.

The team has been located in 'Lemon Arbour' and, now the wives have arrived, we really are beginning to resemble a Caribbean Coronation Street. It is a little warren of cricketing couples, everybody rocking into everybody else's outside patio for early morning tea, elevenses or pre-prandial sun-downers. I find it a much more natural, normal and pleasant environment than the Hilton in Trinidad with its combination of American prices, Third World service, and churlish behaviour. There is no doubt that everyone is so much happier since the girls appeared. Misogynists of the T.C.C.B., please take note.

Barbados is, perhaps, the most 'British' of all Caribbean islands, and shows no signs of the French and Spanish cultures which have permeated other English-speaking islands. The first British expedition landed here in 1625, and by 1640 sugar cane was introduced. Barbados' planters were the first in the Caribbean to establish large sugar plantations, and these demanded the importation of vast numbers of African slaves. This led inexorably to a preponderantly Negro population, but until well into the 20th century all political and economic power was wielded by a small white minority. Fortunately, the respect for British political and parliamentary traditions was deep-rooted, so that the eventual transfer of power from one section of the population to the other occurred without trauma. Indeed, the achievement of political independence in 1966 had little effect on the general community, and today Barbados is an independent state within the Commonwealth, with the Governor General, Sir Hugh Springer, representing the Queen. There are, as in the United Kingdom, two Houses of Parliament, and the leader of the Barbados Labour Party, Bernard St John, is currently Prime Minister.

The Barbados Labour Party has been in power for the past ten years and despite the somewhat misleading appellation is probably the most conservative government in the Caribbean. Observers have been quick to notice that with the possible exception of Trinidad (the Trinis are well known for being the exception to any West Indian rule) the more conservative the government the more welcome they have made the England team, Rebs and all. Mr Bernard St John has been one of the few Prime Ministers to take a totally unambiguous and unequivocal stand in favour of the Tour. He knows all too well which side his country's economic bread is buttered, and the arrival of 5,000 English hard-currency-laden tourists to watch the Third Test is not the sort of statistic his tiny island can afford to ignore.

A mere 21 miles long and 14 miles wide, Barbados is a relatively flat, beach-fringed, coral island, and the mainstay of the economy is indubitably the tourist industry. Sugar cane (from which sugar, molasses and Barbados fine rum are produced), sea island cotton, light industry including the manufacture of textiles and computer components, fruit, vegetables, diary produce and fish all contribute to a fair degree of diversification. Barbados can now also produce enough crude oil commercially to supply about one-third of the island's energy requirements, and all in all is generally considered to boast an unequalled record of political and economic stability in the West Indies.

It is probably also the most cricket-crazy Caribbean island, with a more than average quota of 'Bajans' (Barbadians) playing representative cricket for the West Indies. In the pace department Joel Garner and Malcolm Denzil Marshall are two of Barbados' favourite sons. And the well tried and tested West Indian opening batsmen Cuthbert Gordon Greenidge, and Desmond Leo Haynes also hail from the island, as does relative newcomer, Carlisle Alonza Best. Honestly, even the array of forenames is enough to strike fear and trembling into the yeoman heart of many an English Graham, Timothy, David or Ian.

I have always had a bizarre fascination for names, even though combinations of duress, scopolamine, thumb-screws and the census would never extract my second Christian name from me. If ever the Edmonds duo sees fit to extend their recessive genes to progeny, I have sworn to give them all good, straight, classical names: Zeus Edmonds, Aphrodite Edmonds, Poseidon Edmonds and Bacchus Edmonds all have an impressive and suitably apotheosized ring to them.

Lemon Arbour has been more or less cloven into two: at the 'Nursery End', we have the Willeys with six-month-old baby Heather; the Embureys with Clare and new baby Chlöe (she of 'Pampers' fame); the Gooches with blonde, blue-eyed, charmer Hannah; the Willises with Katie-Ann and somehow in the middle of it, Nanny Ian Botham looking after an ailing Les Taylor.

At the other end of the this cricketers' 'Crossroads' we have the couples yet to get off the mark, the band, in biblical terms 'without issue', and those who have — very sensibly — left the issue at home. The Smiths, the Frenches, the Lambs, and Darby and Joan Edmonds are the old married hands scattered in amongst the 'honeymooners'. Alison and Paul Downton, Romany and Neil Foster, Fiona and Richard Ellison, and Patricia and Tim Robinson were all spliced in October of 1985, international cricketing marriages being obliged to slot in between the end of the English season and the beginning of overseas tours.

Lemon Arbour is a perfect paradigm of conjugal bliss; the men clear off to the team room for a post-match drink and talk, and the girls sit around together and pool terrible tales of cricketing marriages: exhausted husbands who don't talk, eat their dinner with never a word of thanks, and fall asleep watching television in total zomboid silence. It is always reassuring to know that everyone is more or less the same.

The girls are still banned from the team room, lest anything vaguely analogous to common sense should infiltrate the men's stratospheric thinking. I have therefore appointed myself the 'Anti-manager', and have established a 'Not the Team Room'. There is a placard to that effect posted neatly on our door:

NOT THE TEAM ROOM
TACTICS AND STRATEGIES STRICTLY PROHIBITED
NOT THE NEXT TEAM MEETINGS
18/4/86
20/4/86
TOPIC (SAME AS TEAM MEETING): WHAT TO DO ON
REST DAY.

Many of the 'Egg and Bacon' brigade would no doubt think me an iconoclast; although judging by some we have seen in Barbados, not all would be familiar with the word.

The inevitable has happened. The men are far more interested in our alternative meetings than in their own redundant and repetitive tripe. Platitudes such as 'those not playing are even more important than those playing', and 'whenever you're batting, look at the scoreboard and add two to the number of players down', and 'a Test Match is five days out of your life' do not bear excessive reiteration. Alternatively, of course, if the entire England team could be encouraged to stay up all night fasting, chanting such axioms 'Mantra-fashion', and psyching themselves into either a catatonic trance or a furious frenzy, such meetings might not be so absolutely superfluous. Tour-issue sackcloth and ashes might not be a bad idea either, not only as penance for such feeble performances in the first two tests, but in an effort to generate some much needed aggression in the Third. In the meantime, until a Jesuit, Ian MacGregor or myself is brought in to reorganize this side, five minute pep talks and optional fielding practice is just not enough to beat the best in the world.

England started this leg by putting themselves at yet another psychological disadvantage by losing the regional match against Barbados. Many observers commented on the apparent aberration inherent in 'resting ' Gower, Gooch, and Lamb for this game. It is not as if anyone has done sufficient to sit on their laurels, and many people felt that they could well have done with the additional match practice. It is only fair to adduce the opposite argument, of course, and plead that all members of the squad should be given the odd game to avoid becoming depressed and match-stale.

The cause you espouse depends very much on whether you feel England should be a galvanized, potentially Test Match winning team or just another philanthropic sporting society. Struggling and failing as the best players currently are, even the most clueless observer would assume they should be grasping every opportunity to improve.

The third One-day International was an unqualified

disaster for England. How the euphoria of the second One-day game in Trinidad, with Graham Gooch's brilliant match-winning performance was allowed to evaporate so soon, and how it was never harnessed into a more positive and optimistic team approach is a phenomenon difficult to fathom. Thus far Phil has not played in any of the One-day games. 'Best bowler in India and Australia last year,' he muses philosophically, 'and not even twelfth man now'. Ostensibly, he appears unconcerned yet deep-down he desperately misses the buzz of being the lynch-pin, of constantly being in the midst of the action: he is frustrated at his overnight relegation to the periphery of these One-day thrashes.

Whether or not his currently strained back would stand up to the fielding rigours of the limited over knock-about is, however, another matter. Few cricketers, it would appear, are normally one hundred per cent physically fit. Usually they are playing with some minor ache, pain or niggle, although chronic complaints are of course much more worrying. Phil is at present obliged to take constant doses of 'Distalgesic', an extremely strong pain-killer. One is sufficient for most human beings: two would fell a horse: and Phil is up to eight a day. The long-term effect of such patent abuse remains to be seen. Certainly, I hold these mega-doses of Distalgesic responsible for some of Phil's less endearing behaviour. One minute he can be unctuously oleaginating his way around the Governor General's cocktail party like some smarmy left-arm oil-slick, and the next minute he can be erupting in some Olympian rage over one of my perhaps not entirely innocuous remarks.

Certainly, Phil seems more and more frustrated with developments on this tour. He perceives a lack of determination and leadership which together have whittled away that bull-dog spirit so prevalent in India, a tour equally as hard and arduous in its own way. The spirit in this touring team was wrong from the outset. It is certainly difficult to avoid the impression that the team was weakened from the very beginning: by players who made no secret of the fact that they wanted to go home from the outset, and by characters who were grasping at the many political straws to have the entire tour called off. Why they made themselves available for selection and agreed to come in the first instance is not totally incomprehensible. Firstly, none of them is capable of doing anything other than playing cricket in any event. And secondly, refusal to do battle with the best in the world might, in fairness, have precluded automatic selection for a relatively easy New Zealand and India home season ride. Despite some of the blanket criticism that is being meted out to the team in the English press, it certainly looks to me as if just a few, bad, ultra-selfish apples are spoiling an otherwise genuinely enthusiastic barrel. More of this later, when I've had a chance to phone my publisher's libel lawyers . . .

The tour has certainly brightened up for me since the cricketing consorts arrived. Most of the team have hired Mini Mokes as a fun mode of transport around the island. They are indeed ideal vehicles for bald people with suicidal tendencies, and have the same buzz-factor as a week's non-stop session of Russian Roulette. On the first day's hire, the windscreen of one suddenly fell on to Ian Botham and Les Taylor's laps, splintering them with glass. The next day, Ian's brakes failed, and the thing went careering into a wall. Poor old Botham. It would *have* to happen to him. The gear-stick of mine came away somewhat disconcertingly in my hand as I was trying to reverse in Bridgetown. It was then I decided that I had had quite enough fun for one day, and we hired a nice bourgeois Nissan saloon for the rest of our stay. At around £175 per week, a Moke is not cheap, and the servicing done by some Bajan Rental companies is distressingly desultory.

A plastic convertible soup-can on wheels, a Mini Moke is more the plaything of a trainee kamikaze pilot than of a sensible tourist, and some wag was even brought to draw the analogy between it and the England Cricket team: holes in the side, flapping at the top, and a total lack of direction. He might also have added, and about to explode. The word is out that Graham Gooch is about to make another cosmic communiqué to the world.

The Third Test was . . . Sadly, I'm running out of adjectives to convey the degree of depressed fatalism which seems to be permeating many of the team, especially the upper and middle order batsmen.

I arrived on the first day to watch the start of play. This in itself was no mean achievement, given some truly outrageous Moke driving from Alison Downton (who did not give much indication of wanting to see her first wedding anniversary); some pretty hysterically ribald South African commentary on the state of the Barbadian nation from Lindsay Lamb; and some uncontrollably dirty giggles from Fiona Ellison and myself squeezed tightly in the back. Momentarily stopped at the lights, some big, black buck made Lindsay an offer that her Cape Town upbringing did not find desperately difficult to refuse, and off we roared to the Kensington Oval, Bridgetown.

Team selection had been facilitated by the fact that there were only 12 fit men. Good old Mike 'Call Me Gritty' Gatting is back with us after a fairly nasty and complicated operation to rebuild his nose. He is such a stalwart, gutsy, positive and aggressive man: a real bull terrier. One can only hope that this 'never say die' attitude communicates itself to less enthusiastic players as the few remaining weeks go by. It was a sad misfortune that he had his thumb broken in the territorial match between Barbados and England.

I met him after my early morning swim in Lemon Arbour, and he was as jovially good-humoured and buoyant as ever.

'How's the thumb?' I asked.

'Oh, it's just a knock,' he replied, showing me a really ugly bruised, black nail. 'Only one more thing to happen now. They say misfortunes come in threes.' He was off to practice, broken nose, broken thumb and all.

'Gatt,' opined Tony Brown, impressed, 'apart from anything, is worth his place on guts alone, and the contribution he makes to team spirit.' And who in all honesty could gainsay that?

It would not be difficult to fault Gatt's common sense and instincts of self-preservation in returning so soon to face this incredibly fast West Indian music, but you couldn't fault his loyalty and determination. His nose seems to have healed up remarkably quickly, a tell-tale horizontal scar on the bridge and some residual swelling being the only outward manifestations of the entire Marshall affair.

'Do you like it better than your last one?' quizzed Fiona Ellison, concerned, reviewing the cosmetic surgery critically, as if cricketers acquired a new one every tour. The psychological scars, if any, remain to be seen.

If the England Team corridor in the Trinidad Hilton looked like *Emergency Ward 10*, the Rockley Resort is starting to resemble *Apocalypse Now*. Regular cricket correspondents are beginning to realize that a copy of *Gray's Anatomy* is more useful in compiling their Test Match previews than any number of statistic-stuffed *Wisdens*.

Les Taylor has been laid low by some non-specific lergy. Already deaf in one ear, he has apparently now gone temporarily deaf in both, which is probably no bad thing when you're sharing a room with 'Beefy' Botham. I wanted to take him a bottle of Johnnie Walker Black Label whisky, and a dose of own-brand female solace, but Phil generously assured me that I was the last person a sick man would want to see.

'Take no notice of him next time,' said Les when I eventually explained my absence from his death-bed. 'The Johnnie Walker at least would have been most acceptable.'

David Smith is still suffering from a back injury sustained in Trinidad, and Richard Ellison has some vague viral complaint. By the rest day, Tim Robinson had gone down with a bad attack of 24-hour 'flu. And in the Women's Ward many of the girls are still suffering from an assortment of imported English winter ailments. Fiona Ellison, having sung herself hoarse in an 'Am-Dram' production of Gilbert and Sullivan's *The Gondoliers* has taken to gargling with Harvey's Bristol Cream Sherry. ('Julie Andrews does it. Why shouldn't I?') Phil too has now contracted a sore throat, and has taken to gargling with our rather expensive Hine Vieille Fine Champagne antique cognac. ('Fiona Ellison does it. Why shouldn't I?') Romany Foster is suffering from 'flu. Alison Downton has a sore throat and a bad eye, and Lindsay Lamb has a shocking cold and a sore ear. If anyone is interested, I am perfectly well, aware of the degree of sympathy to be extracted from hard-hearted Edmonds in the event of any illness.

The day before the Test match, the local paper carried a report that thirteen of the England squad had been to consult their long-suffering team physiotherapist. Their various complaints and maladies were chronicled, including inexplicably, 'David Gower, Broken Heart' . . .

12

Dreams or nightmares?

Laurie Brown, the team's physiotherapist, having worked with Manchester United footballers, knows a thing or two about peak physical fitness. He admitted to me, half-seriously, that a brief perusal of the England cricket team's medical records before he undertook his current task had almost persuaded him to throw in the pre-tour sponge. Fortunately for the players, his Scottish common sense did not prevail over his humanitarian belief in almost totally lost causes, and he has been the busiest, and arguably the best loved man on tour. Beefy Botham refers to him loudly and affectionately as MacDuff, and everyone is genuinely grateful for his tireless efforts on their behalf.

Men in groups can often be very cruel. In a good-natured, bantering sort of way, everyone's shortcomings on tour, everyone's foibles, deep dark secrets, or embarrassing moments are common property and liable to mirth. If you happen to be thin, fat, bald, black, South African, hung-over, a Middlesex player or having a tempestuous affair with an ex-Miss Trinidad — anything and everything is potentially joke material. It is an indication of the fondness that the boys feel for Laurie, that no-one has ever so much as mentioned problems of his former marriage. The female contingent unanimously decided, over banana daiquiris in our 'Not The Team Meeting' that there is no accounting for taste.

The Kensington Oval is not a pretty ground, although vast efforts are currently being deployed to improve and renovate it. We were seated in the Garfield Sobers Pavilion, and we all agreed it was one of the 'most exciting and interesting day's cricket ever'. Mick Jagger was seated two rows behind.

The majority of the crowd was composed of English tourists, many of the 5,000 who had come to Barbados specifically to watch the Test Match. To watch these pitiful pilgrims sizzling like the whites of so many over-fried eggs, accumulating third-degree burns on bare backs and 'I-spent-February-in-England' legs was painful to behold. Some were seated outside the famous 'Three Ws Stand' (Walcott, Weekes, and Worrell, three famous West Indian cricketers), and spent all day wilting in the cauldron heat. I spoke to some supporters who were bitterly disappointed that their cricket tour operators had brought them out on extremely expensive holidays, only to provide them with totally unacceptable seating arrangements. It is probably wise to check on that kind of ostensibly minor, but effectively major, consideration before handing over the two, three or four thousand-pound-for-a-fortnight's-cricket-watching cheque.

A couple of people passed out with sun-stroke, but a few, sporting Essex Country Cricket Club logobilia on their heads and incandescent heat blisters on their backs, were happily downing bottles of Bank's beer as if it were merely a warmish sort of day at Chelmsford, and by lunchtime were feeling no pain. For less anaesthetized supporters, it was probably an uncomfortable if salutary lesson in understanding how the professionals feel after a day in the field under tropical conditions.

Bruce French, the reserve wicketkeeper and acting twelfth man, brought us all coffee for elevenses. It is difficult to speak too highly of Bruce. It is no easy job to be away on tour for three months and know for a fact that, barring injury to the first wicketkeeper, you are not likely to play in any of the international games. It is easy to get bored, listless, depressed and lazy. Bruce is not in that mould. He seems to have a degree of personal self-reliance which some of the others would do well to emulate. His spare time is spent mountain climbing, and painstakingly reconstructing his Nottinghamshire village home, stone by stone. He and his wife, Ellen, certainly are human dynamos, with boundless physical energy, a 'try-anything-once' approach, and an infectious *joie de vivre*. 'Froggie French' has yet to earn his first England cap, and while not wanting to see Paul Downton dropped, everyone would be pleased to see Froggie receive his colours. There is, sadly, only one wicketkeeping spot per team.

Bruce came to fetch us for lunch after the teams had finished. Inexplicably, my mind was focused on whether the derivation of 'crumbs from the rich man's table' was Old or New Testament, or indeed somewhere else entirely.

The dining room was next to the two teams' dressing rooms. It was not that I objected in any way to the all too familiar acrid amalgam of sweaty cricket socks, rancid jock straps and horse liniment whilst I surveyed the detritus of the England and West Indian rice and peas. It was merely overcome by a sudden and unexpected nostalgia for that NW8 navel of the universe, the mecca of the handle-bar moustache and the 'golf-ball-in-the-gob' old Etonian accent. Lord's, and more specifically the hospitality tent at Lord's, where a judicious fiver to an accommodating waitress at lunchtime guarantees a perfectly potable white Bordeaux until stumps. Lord's, with half the Cabinet neatly 'paired' with half the shadow cabinet in the Pavilion, the level of debate comfortingly more fatuous than even the House of Commons. Lord's, where the petrified gargoyle 'Grace' gatemen refuse to recognize the mere Middlesex mortals, and belligerently protect that M.C.C. Ark of the Covenant from all but the 'Egg and Bacon' talisman-toting few. Lord's, that last bastion of male chauvinism, that High Church of arch conservatism, that epitome of anti-feminism. Lord's, all is forgiven. Just never change those Test Match outside caterers.

The Barbados Test was all but wrapped up in three days, with England again on the brink of a humiliating innings defeat. The fourth day was to be the rest day, and so the local board of control invited both teams for an evening cruise aboard the *Bajan Queen*. It was, putatively, going to be a quiet little affair: the England team, the West Indian team, a few hand-selected members of the press, a couple of the Cable and Wireless sponsors, one or two members of the Test and County Cricket Board, and the West Indian Board of Control.

The West Indians had obviously played before, and with the signal exceptions of Courtney Walsh and Carlisle Best (presumably too young to know better) and Desmond Haynes, pleaded sea-sickness, aversion to rum punch and an inalienable attachment to *terra firma*. The England team, with a few notable absences, arrived horrified to discover a rather naff little vessel, bursting at the seams and submerged to the very Plimsoll line, sporting a jolly 400 strong cargo of merrymakers of variegated hues and states of inebriation, utterly intent on an ear-bashing good time.

But for the cajoling insistence of the 'well, we're all dressed-up-so-we-may-as-well-go' wives, the England team would gladly have turned heel and fled. As it was the girls insisted the show go on, and those who went thoroughly enjoyed themselves, with the open bar, the barbecue dinner of steak, chicken and the delicious local 'Flying fish', and the disco bopping.

Phil and I met two psychiatrists. Strange how we attract that sort of person. The Irish psychiatrist, a man presumably paid to drive people nuts (and with a maiden name like Moriarty, only I can make that kind of joke), advanced his theories on the England team's current attitude. He perceived abject defeatism in the very manner in which they were walking to the wicket. Batsmen, he remarked, were leaving the pavilion with their heads stooped and their bats almost dragging behind them. Psychologically they were geared to lose. He continued to adduce his own subtle reasons for the phenomenon. Was there a lack of leadership? Was there any clear-cut strategy or tactics? Did each member of the management team have clear 'job-definition'? Was the captain too nice? Was a stronger line needed with non 'line-towers'? Was a team 'supremo' a good concept, somebody to take full and absolute control of cricket and cricketers on and off the pitch, some sort of sporting benevolent dictator?

The French psychiatrist, a lady, was equally effete; what were the basic qualities intrinsic to leadership? Did 'nice-ness' have anything to do with it? Leading a winning team was easy, what kind of man was necessary to turn defeat to success, or at least to stop the rot? Was anyone in the management charged with the task of motivation? If not, why not? What was the ineffable gift of natural authority, and who in the present England team had it? And — *nom de dieu* — what had happened to all those nice public school and Oxbridge types? (That, *ma chère Madame Psychiatre*, is the very question I should most like answered.) It was, alto-gether, a profoundly deep and meaningful experience.

'Well,' said the Irish psychiatrist rather pleased with him-self, as we wound up our interfacing session, 'in my pro-fessional capacity as a consultant psychiatrist, people would have to pay 50 guineas an hour to hear that kind of positive advice.'

'Well,' I thought, in a mental parry and thrust, 'in my pro-fessional capacity as a conference interpreter, people would have to pay me fifty guineas an hour to listen to that kind of verbal pounding.'

The psychiatrists, nevertheless, did seem to have put the professional finger on the problem. While many of the popu-lar press are busy muck-raking for every conceivable extran-eous reason for loss of form (sex, drugs, rock'n'roll), only a few of the more perceptive have grasped the real nettle. There is simply no authoritative leadership on this tour.

'And who, ma chère Françoise,' asked our French lady psychiatrist at her most lucidly Cartesian, 'who exactly runs zees T.C.C.B.?'

The next day was the rest day. Inevitably, as in Trinidad, it poured. With the tiniest bit of gentle prodding from yours truly, the General Manager of the Rockley, Barry Burns, 'spontaneously' suggested a champagne breakfast for the Honeymooners, around our own semi-private Lemon Arbour swimming pool. There is no motivation like self-interest, and neither in this life is there any 'quid' without a 'pro quo'. The general manager wanted a bit of publicity for his resort, and I wanted to do a colour feature for Eddie Shah's new paper *Today*. All that was necessary was a few group photographs to be taken by Adrian Murrell, and the champers could flow.

The whole episode was a distressing indication of how low press — player relations have sunk. Initially, Tim Robinson and Paul Downton, in particular, seemed uneasy at having any photograph taken which in any way showed them enjoying themselves.

The camera, so the adage runs, tells no lies, but the sort of story which accompanies the photo can tell just about any tale. Fun shots Adrian had taken of Ian Botham and David Gower enjoying themselves on a boat whilst England were playing their first warm-up match against the Windward Islands in St Vincent had been transformed by journalists into anything other than innocuous. Had England been beating the lowly Windwards, the accompanying caption could well have read: 'England captain and Leukaemia-walk hero take well deserved rest before the big one'. As it happened, England slumped to an embarrassingly unexpected defeat, and captions were reading along the lines of: 'Where are England's captain and best player while England's boat sinks?' It remains, incidentally, to be seen whether either of those two appellations weather the storm of this tour, but the point is clear. A photograph may be perfectly innocent, but attendant copy can make it totally damning.

Alison Downton, in particular, had eminently good reason to be suspicious of anything to do with press and photographers. A snap of David Gower giving her a congratulatory peck on the cheek during the reception when she and

Paul were married was what had encouraged some creature from the gutter press to crawl out of the skirting boards of Fleet Street and ring her up early in the tour. He suggested — with an imagination as vivid as his approach was sordid — that she and David were having an affair, thus accounting for David's inexplicable loss of form. As if cricket widows did not have enough to put up with without that type of scandal-mongering. The Press Council really should be encouraged to take a harder line with these appalling examples of journalistic filth. There are absolutely no depths to which they will not stoop. But more of the press and media later . . .

Eventually, after my personal guarantees and assurances, Adrian's promises of full-colour prints, and the general manager's 'come hither' proclivity with champagne corks, the entire Honeymoon contingent was happily mustered, and very much enjoyed their convivial, conjugal champagne breakfast.

There was no way such a bibulous event was going to remain the exclusive bailiwick of the newly-wed Ellisons, Fosters, Robinsons and Downtons. Other members of the team soon congregated. 'Francisco,' shouted Allan Lamb, with the not entirely (I like to think) unaffectionate misnomer he applies to me. 'If this party is for newly-weds, what is an old stick of biltong like you doing here?' (Biltong, for the gastronomically uninitiated, is a South African speciality of wind-dried meat. It is dark brown, crinkly, and comes in long, thin, slivers. The appositeness of the metaphor will not be lost on those who know and love me.)

A group of about twenty of us spent the rest of the day in the patrician lap of naval luxury aboard the *Welsh Princess*. The multi-millionaire owner, Chris Bailey, has two particularly endearing attributes: bags of style, and the loot to do something about it. He anchored in Bridgetown and immediately rang up the British High Commissioner, Sir Giles Bullard. Where, Chris wanted to know, was the English cricket team, and would they like to come for a day's cruise? I contracted the distinct impression that evening over dinner with Sir Giles and his American wife, Linda, that a more lively Bailey interest in the whereabouts and *desiderata* of the British High Commission might not have met with an entirely total deflection either, but sadly, such is life. The England team alone was welcome.

The *Welsh Princess* is one of a fleet of yachts owned by Dragon Yachts (Worldwide) Limited, a Cardiff based company specializing in private luxury cruises. We were shown around the gorgeous staterooms, one with mirrors decorating the entire ceiling, presumably designed for ladies who like to watch themselves having a headache. The yacht can accommodate eight to eighteen guests on board, and if you have seven to seventeen friends, and a couple of grand a day to spare, this must be the way to cruise the Caribbean. It was on this wonderful vessel that Agatha Christie's thriller *Death on the Nile* was filmed, but I unsportingly refused to be 'done in' merely to accommodate Phil's burgeoning Belgian desire to play a latter-day, left-arm, orthodox Hercule Poirot.

Ian Botham inevitably located a 'Guy the Gorilla' outfit, and the hope of any post-prandial peace was lost. The weather was unfortunately overcast and drizzling, but normally, days on board can be spent wind-surfing, scuba diving, power boat racing in the Rivas, fishing, ballooning, para-kiting or, for the more sybaritic, merely eating, drinking and sitting in the steaming jacuzzi on deck. Eighteen of us piled into it and fervently hoped for the best.

'It's what you dream of in Manchester,' sighed our resident Caledonian, 'Macduff', pushing Beefy Botham's mysteriously bandaged foot out of his mouth. 'What you *dream* of . . .' It certainly beat our somewhat more plebeian passage on the *Bajan Queen* and its day-time equivalent, *The Jolly Roger*. Walking the plank, rope swinging and pirate weddings are fun for some in this Caribbean Clacton-on-Sea, but rather give me a tall 175 foot private ship, and a star to steer her by.

That evening Phil and I had dinner with the Secretary of

the West Indian Board of Control, Steve Camacho, his wife Alison, and our friend from Jamaica, Patrick Rousseau. It is tragic that some of the less enthusiastic English tourists have never come out of their navel-contemplating seclusion long enough to meet such people and properly to comprehend the Herculean efforts which have been deployed to salvage this tour.

The majority of the Prime Ministers of CARICOM (the Caribbean Community of past and present English colonies) were at first violently opposed to the inclusion of South African Rebels in the England team and only the tireless public relations exercise carried out by cricket authorities and lovers in general, and ex-Jamaican Prime Minister, Michael Manley, in particular, saved the series.

Phil was batting next morning and wanted an early night. Patrick started to regale us with Bacchanalian tales of his great friend Sir Garfield Sobers (Sobie), who would carouse till 6 am down Baxter Street, Barbados, and have a double century on the board by tea-time. In an impassioned exhibition of 'Devil-may-care' brinkmanship, Phil ordered a single cognac and stayed up till way past ten o'clock. He was out second ball the next day.

England suffered a humiliating innings defeat, and the game was over by lunch on the fourth day. Everyone was desperately depressed, not least of all members of the West Indian Board of Control who are losing revenue hand over fist because of these truncated Tests.

Wednesday and Thursday were proclaimed rest days, and so Phil and I set off to tour the island. First of all we visited the Barbados Wildlife Reserve, which is definitely worth a detour to miss. For the paltry sum of £10 we managed to catch a glimpse of two fornicating Green Monkeys, and one demented tortoise walking slowly around in ever decreasing circles. Contemplation of his own posterior was evidently more interesting than the galling spectacle of monkeys having a good time. Earlier we had passed the Barbados Primate Research Centre, to which entry was barred. I am

convinced they are engaged in some Patrick Patterson clon-
ing exercise, or genetically engineering an entire West Indian
squad of Viv Richards look-and-play-alikes.

I watched Patrick Patterson very carefully at breakfast
when we stayed in the Trinidad Hilton. Breakfast there is a
help-yourself buffet, which in that particular hotel is a verita-
ble godsend, since nobody else is even half inclined to help
you. Patrick has muscles in places where other men simply
do not have places. I made a mental note of what he was
eating. Perhaps England's failures are down to dietary problems. God knows, the press have adduced every other conceivable reason. Were the West Indians at some culinary
advantage over us?

First of all Patrick selected a box of Kellog's *Special K*.
Couldn't be that. And besides, with those 90 miles per hour
smell-the-leather 'perfumed balls' rocketing past their noses
the England team are certainly not in need of any extra
roughage. He then collected (could my early-morning eyes
have been deceiving me?) a plate of raw minced meat.

'Don't be silly, Frances,' said Phil. 'It's hash.'

Well, Phil can continue to think what he likes, but I am
persuaded that they are feeding that boy raw meat. I then
helped him do battle with a recalcitrant toaster and told
him (in my school ma'am Mistress Edmonds sort of voice)
to keep his fingers out of it. Shucks! Missed my chance to
serve our Queen and country. I can see the headlines
now. 'England spinner's wife conflagrates West Indian
pace-man'.

Our tour of Barbados brought us to Harrison's Cave,
which really was worth the visit. We boarded the special train
for the mile-long cave trip, marvelling at the subterranean
streams, waterfalls, cascades, pools, stalagmites and stalac-
tites. Strange aggregations of stalagmites looked uncannily
like colonies of petrified people. The folk in front of us, some
of the 5,000 strong cricketing supporters deprived of their
fifth day's play, recognized Phil, and leaned into a huddled
muttering conclave as to what to do about it. Eventually one,

plucking up courage, turned around and took a photograph. Another asked for an autograph 'for Beryl in the office'. It must be wonderful, being famous.

The east coast of the island is picturesquely rugged, with Atlantic breakers pounding in, ideal for body surfing and breaking your neck. We visited Sam Lord's Castle, an elegant Georgian mansion now turned resort hotel, originally built in 1820 by the famous buccaneer, Samuel Lord Hall. Many of the priceless antiques which this gentleman plundered from the luckless passing ships are still on display in the castle. At the nearby Crane Beach Beefy Botham has been keeping his adrenaline high by diving, Acapulco-style, off the mountains into the raging surf below. After three Tests facing the blistering West Indian pace attack on the field, and the excoriating excesses of the British press off, such antics must have seemed as innocuous as paddling along the front in Blackpool.

The west coast is washed by the more calm and quiet Caribbean waters. Ultra-expensive hotels overlook glorious palm-fringed, white sand, coral beaches leading down to the clear blue tepid sea. One such hotel, Coconut Creek, hosted a reception for the two teams before the One-day International. There was a three line whip that night, so all the boys were obliged to turn up. Those with wives confined to barracks with children retreated as soon as was decently possible, however. It really cannot have been much of a holiday for the families with youngsters.

Les Taylor, as usual, had us in fits. Phil was getting a pretty fearful ear-bashing from a dreadfully tedious limpet-like supporter. I honestly don't know what promises some of these cricket tour operators make in their brochures, but a few supporters really do appear to think that their package includes the fully paid-up right to pester the players at any time of the day or night. One such character had phoned David Gower at six in the morning when we had arrived in Trinidad for the Second Test. It had been a galling eight-hour flight from Jamaica, with four stops and two bomb scares. David, after an obligatory talk to the press, had managed to get to bed at 3 am.

'Good morning,' came the chirpy little early morning voice. 'I'm ringing up to wish you luck.'

David's answer was apparently encapsulated in two monosyllabic words. They were not, by all accounts, 'thank you'.

A similar individual attached himself to Phil at the cocktail party. Les 'call me d'Artagnan' Taylor saw his friend in need, and rallied to his support.

'Good evening, Mr Edmonds,' he said. 'I've always wanted to meet you. May I shake you by the hand? It really is an honour, you know. Would you mind coming over here to sign my autograph book?'

After the two rest days, a session of optional practice was organized for the Friday. There were, as Lindsay Lamb commented, more press than players at the nets, and it was perhaps not entirely good psychology that the England captain, David Gower, failed to show up. Comprehensively thrashed in three successive Tests, a show of public penance to mollify the media was certainly necessary. Far worse. Not only did David fail to show up, but he was actually out enjoying himself windsurfing. The fact that the nets were washed out by torrential rain was irrelevant. The Press vampires were after David's blood. It was a question of being *seen* to be doing the right thing, whether the right thing was useful or not. From now on, incidentally, practice is compulsory.

It is unfortunate that practice facilities in the West Indies have not always been up to scratch, and have often been an almost total waste of time. The 'Goat Field' in St Vincent and the 'Cow Patch' in Antigua bear eloquent testimony to the state of some of the pitches.

Even more serious has been the condition of some of the Test Match tracks. The England manager, Tony Brown, felt obliged to address an unofficial letter of complaint to the Secretary of the West Indian Board of Control, Steve Camacho, adverting particularly to 'Uneven Bounce'. Similarly esoteric considerations are not, of course, for such an uninitiated layperson as myself to comment upon. I had always fondly assumed that 'uneven bounce' was a phenomenon evidenced by buxom matrons who had failed to adjust their 'Cross Your Heart Bras' correctly. The net result in both instances is not totally dissimilar. An unsuspecting gent is more than likely to get one in the face.

In writing his letter, Tony no doubt felt that he was merely reflecting the feelings of the entire England team. Three Tests down, however, missives of such a nature are distressingly liable to be misconstrued as whingeing. Neither were observers slow to level the counter charge that West Indian batsmen had been playing on exactly the same pitches, and not really making such a bad job of it. Far better, perhaps, to keep a stiff upper English lip until this particularly perilous party is over.

The press, deprived of entire days of cricket, are struggling to concoct stories, and any lunatic idea is now given currency. Some disgruntled Nottinghamshire supporter delivered a letter to Keith Walcott, a member of the Barbados Board of Control, and brother of the famous West Indian batsman, Clive. The import of the letter was fairly clear. England's present distress could be attributed to the omission of the Nottinghamshire batsman, Derek Randall, the failure to play Nottinghamshire wicket keeper, Bruce French, and the fact that the Middlesex 'clique' was in almost open revolt against the beleaguered captain, David Gower. The Middlesex contingent (Mike Gatting, Paul Downton, Phil Edmonds, John Emburey, and replacement Wilf Slack) all found this highly amusing and, whenever rumours like this are given press credence, the players start to play-act as if they were true.

'May I have a word with you?' David asked Phil one morning.

'I'm afraid, Captain, you'll have to go through the Middlesex contingent's secretariat. Proper channels you know. All requests and questions in triplicate.'

The misogynists, naturally, are having a field day. Well,

let us get this semantically correct. These gentlemen of the press do not hate *all* women. They seem to find no objection to the multitudes of groupies and assorted bits of fluff that congregate like tumbleweed around any touring party. No. That sort of woman is perfectly welcome. It is only the appearance of the *bona fide* wives and consorts which is liable to criticism. Honestly, the way these people are talking, you would think England had been thrashing the West Indies in Kingston and Port of Spain, and that a sudden disintegration occurred when the distaff element tipped up in Barbados.

Some correspondents have even been blaming the wives for the husbands' failure to turn up to the 'optional' practice sessions which was certainly unfair. And no one has actually bothered to mention that perhaps the persistently worst and most obvious offender did not even have his wife in Barbados. Furthermore, it has been alleged that the presence of the 'loved ones' has been yet another divisive element in an already fragmented and 'clique' ridden team. Nothing could be further from the truth. If anything, the girls tended to create a more cohesive and convivial collective. The boys would leave their fruitlessly repetitive team meetings (the younger and keener players being perfectly sick of the disruptive 'I've played in 80 Test Matches and I've heard all this shit before' element), and join us in our 'Not the Team' meeting. It was there, believe it or not, that Phil, Paul Downton, Richard Ellison, Neil Foster, Allan Lamb, David Smith, Tim Robinson and Bruce French would often do their most sensible and constructive cricket talking.

The Downtons and the Lambs, dab hands with the barbecue, did a lot of good in moulding the team together with evening sessions broiling over the charcoal. Indeed, the warren of rabbit hutches' existence in the Kingston Pegasus and the Trinidad Hilton, ideal for the formation of cliques and neuroses, was totally dismantled in the Rockley, Barbados. Not only were the members of the team far happier and more emotionally stable and content, but the actual group ethic was certainly stronger there than it had been anywhere else on tour.

As I've already said, the press are genuinely struggling to find just any reason on which to blame England's failures. The very correspondents who are currently cavilling at the presence of wives in the Caribbean, and who bunch into such high encomiums about the wonderful morale and team-spirit which so hallmarked the victorious England team on last year's India tour seem to have forgotten that Fiona Ellison, Lindsay Lamb, Alison Downton, Patricia Robinson and I were all out there as well, with no apparently deleterious effect on the team. It is, in any event, churlishly irrational to suggest that wives should be banned from these four-month relationship-straining hauls.

If a player feels he is prepared to pay give-or-take £1,500 to see his wife for a fortnight, then no one, not even the most egregious members of the T.C.C.B. and the press corps, should have the temerity to comment on it. Just too many bloody bachelors in this game.

Australian Kerry Packer, who unlike the darling amateur bumblers of the T.C.C.B. is a real professional and a hard businessman, organized accommodation for all his 'Circus' players' wives, and crèches and nannies for their children. Psychologically more astute than his establishment counterparts he understood that most players, to perform at their very best, must be emotionally secure, content and happy, and this generally involves having the stability of a family environment.

John Jackson of the *Daily Mirror* was impressed in an interview to hear Graham Gooch's extraordinarily eloquent defence of wives and children on tour. He certainly seems less prickly when Brenda, his wife, is with him. And my heart positively warmed to the man when I saw him taking their darling, blonde, blue-eyed daughter Hannah for a walk around the swimming pool. A tiny tot, and 'Daddy's little girl' she was wearing Graham's Rastafarian-coloured sweat bands around her chubby wrists. They really made an adorable picture. People in Graham's confidence even suggest that it is his love of domestic life that has made him apparently unkeen on touring. Perhaps the T.C.C.B. should start thinking in terms of sponsoring wives on these three, four and five month stints, and never mind banning them.

To be absolutely fair, there *are* players who are not enthusiastic about having either their own wife or indeed anybody else's on tour, and they have not been slow in telling me. It is true, of course, that they do get a lot more practice in than the others. It is not, unfortunately, always in the nets.

Incidentally, I almost forgot, there is, and has been since the outset, an extremely pretty bevvy of West Indian wives following the cricket from island to island. This, oh misogynists of the British press, would presumably account for *their* team's shambolic performance; of course, the basic problem on this tour is that there are far too many correspondents out here trying to justify their vast expenses, and not enough real news to write about. The entire three-month story would be neatly embraced in a couple of extremely short sentences. England has been outbowled, outbatted, and outfielded by the best cricket team in the world. The West Indians are simply in a different league to everybody else. Speculation on, and permutation of reasons why we are losing is almost as redundant as wondering why Frances Edmonds does not run as fast as Sebastian Coe. We are just not good enough.

Sadly, by this stage the cricket seems to have become the topic of least news value, and every facet of players' personal and private lives is constantly under the media microscope. More, much more, of this later . . .

No one, but no one, was happy to leave Barbados. Lindsay Lamb, Alison Downton, and David Gower's fiancée, Vicki, continued on to Antigua. They had obviously heard about Trinidad. The other wives flew home to the bitter British weather, their lovingly nurtured sun-tans soon to fade under the April showers. I shall miss them all desperately: Romany Foster's 'nothing to give Nancy Lopez the Yips about' golf shots; Fiona Ellison's infectiously gurgling giggle and

Lindsay Lamb's roving South African ambassador in Barbados blasphemy and her hysterical entrepreneurial activities.

The 'Lindsay's Loopy Lug' Empire, *à propos*, is in temporary liquidation until she returns from the West Indies, but her line in earrings is something to behold. Poor Allan is given the labourer's job of slicing rubber animals into two, and our craftswoman Lindsay then mounts them as earrings. The effect is a disconcerting impression of animals running straight through the wearer's head. Just the sort of thing for High Commission cocktail parties and Governor General's dos. Anyone who wants further outrageous details should contact the Secretary of Northamptonshire County Cricket Club.

We boarded our transfer bus to the airport and said our fond farewells. 'No tears!' ordered David Gower manfully, but I swear I even saw strong-man Peter Willey sigh as he waved farewell to his six-month-old daughter, Heather. Neil Foster sat in the corner clutching pictures of his boxer dog and his wife. He is such a clean-cut good-looking, nice young man, that Foster. They are all beginning to look so young to me.

We all had to be very silent on the bus. Beefy Botham wanted to listen to the English football results being broadcast on the radio. Not a word was spoken, lest we should miss the crucial details of Scunthorpe Football Club's performance.

'And Cambridge,' added the pukka BBC voice, 'has won the boat race.'

'Hurrah!' chorused Phil and I, in light blue fervour.

'Bloody snobs,' said the rest of the bus.

13

Trinidad — again!

Trinidad is a rat-ass country. If you don't believe me, then ask the West Indian opening batsman, Barbadian Desmond Haynes. This is what he said, according to the Trinidadian rag *Sports Update*. I do, however, have it on the excellent authority of the *Birmingham Evening Mail* cricket correspondent, Jack Bannister, that Desmond is feeling horribly misquoted. 'Flea-pit' was apparently the exact expression employed.

Here we are again, immured in our Trinidad Hilton Warren. Phil and I are located next to the West Indian team room, and I spend a lot of time listening with a wine glass to the wall, or hanging surreptitiously over the balcony in Mata Hari attempts to uncover their diabolical tactics. Unfortunately, when they all speak together in some incomprehensible windian patois, it is very difficult to decipher their next demonic strategem. There also seems to be a lot of buoyant, black power, hand-slapping salutes, the reverberations of which are doing absolutely no good whatsoever to the wall or the wine glass.

It is difficult to speak too lowly of the Hilton. Notwithstanding the young maître d'hôtel, a blond, stony-faced Aryan, of aristocratic Prussian manners and clipped Teutonic ways, Germanic concepts of service and discipline do not quite percolate through to the local Trinis in the kitchen. Even the mild-mannered and melifluous John Woodcock (*The Times*) was obliged to pen a letter of complaint on 'The Old Thunderer' headed writing paper to object to the three hour delay in service in the restaurant ('Trinidad's finest' to quote the not-entirely objective Hilton brochure). Objective and courteous as ever, however, 'Wooders' went on to thank the management for the munificent generosity of the freebie Hilton Easter Egg!

I also spend a lot of time avoiding the Reuter's Venezuelan photographer. Poor darling was originally sent from Caracas to cover the Second Test, and Tony Brown introduced him to me last time we were in Trinidad. He neither speaks nor writes a single word of English, and knows absolutely nothing about cricket. In this, at least, he is on a par with many of the press covering the tour. He fell on me like a long lost compatriot, totally deprived as he had been of any conversation or information in Spanish. Tony ('Antonio') had given him a list of names ('Nombres y apellidos') of the England cricket team, but our man from Caracas had presumably experienced some difficulty in correlating names with faces. I should not be in the least surprised if photographs of Edmond Philipps (sic), looking remarkably like Allan Lamb at the crease have been winging their way across the world, together with shots of Paul Downtown (sic) purveying a top-class brand of off-spin. It all seems pretty consistent with the degree of misinformation which has been prevalent this trip. For the Fourth Test, unfortunately, my Venezuelan friend has decided to apprise himself further of the finer nuances of the game, and keeps accosting me with the cricket columns of *The Times* and *The Guardian*, demanding on-the-spot sight translations into the language of Cervantes. I have genuinely tried to do my best (despite the patent lacunae in the idiom) to convey the concepts of 'uneven bounce' and 'turning wickets'. When we got to 'swinging balls', however, my mind turned unaccountably to 'bull-fighting', and pleading a migraine I retired to bed.

A pall of uncertainty is still hanging over the tour. Graham Gooch is known to have given a letter to the Chairman of Selectors, Peter May, on his departure from Barbados, apparently outlining his position with respect to the Deputy Prime Minister of Antigua Lester Bird. As early as the 30th January 1986, Lester Bird issued a statement in response to comments made by the Antiguan Education and Sports Minister, Reuben Harris. To any half-aware observer, the whole affair was nothing more than an internecine domestic squabble, the equivalent of a storm in a Caribbean banana-republic tea cup. Bird had simply stated that in his personal capacity, he would not be attending any of the fixtures in Antigua. He laid into Harris for confusing the issue by erroneously alleging that he (Bird) had been speaking in his capacity as Foreign Minister, and not merely as an individual. Bird then launched into a fairly *ad hominem* attack on the Sports and Education Minister for accusing him of 'undermining his (Harris') sports machinery and programme'. Mr Bird took greatest exception in his statement to the fact that Mr Harris, 'casts the efforts of the entire Antigua Labour Party Government as "His" '. I think from these few snippets, you can readily appreciate the level of discussion. Mr Harris then immediately and inevitably convened a Press Conference to launch a counterattack on Mr Bird. And so, it would seem, they pass their time away in Antigua: two not absolutely internationally significant politicians in an island with the population of Southend trying to score debating points over one another.

Indeed, anyone who cared to read the statement made by Lester Bird aired on Cana radio on Thursday 30th January 1986, with anything other than a totally paranoid, egocentric and navel-contemplating eye would have been obliged to concede that it was nothing more nor less than that. Bird even went so far as to concede:

'The Gleneagles Agreement . . . may bind my Government and me as a minister to accept the England team in this country. But it does not bind me as an individual to watch them play cricket. While I will not attend the test match in Antigua, I do not dictate to anyone what they should do. I act by my conscience, others must act by theirs. It is not my wish that anyone should intimidate or threaten the safety of the players.'

It was all relatively innocuous stuff. Graham Gooch,

however, was apparently angered by Bird criticizing his rebel tour of South Africa in 1982. As Lester Bird stated in the same relatively low-key statement:

'I cannot accept that a simple retraction of a statement is sufficient to wash away the comfort that players in the English side have given to a regime which brutalizes people.'

All this had clearly been festering in Gooch's mind since the team's visit to Antigua for England's territorial match against the Leewards in early February. The running sore of putatively injured pride and hard-done-by attitude was also kept well and truly open by the not entirely responsible antics of one member of the press, which unnecessarily wound Gooch up. Gooch, who had always steadfastly, if somewhat naively, claimed that he never wanted to be involved in politics, and that in going to South Africa he only wanted to ply his trade and play his cricket, was now, rather inconsistently, involved in doing exactly the opposite. Everyone else, however, agreed that it was the exclusive task of the T.C.C.B. and the management to do the statement-making. The players were out there quite simply, as Gooch had so fervently maintained in South Africa, to play cricket. Gooch, therefore, was persuaded to remain silent, and the problem, so it was generally thought, had been neatly and definitively circumvented.

People, however, had underestimated Graham Gooch. The qualities so admirable in an opening batsman: tenacity, stubbornness, the will to fight, never-give-up, and dig-in-the-heels became sadly more in evidence off the field than on. After the Third Test in Barbados, neither Peter May, nor the British High Commissioner of Barbados, Antigua and Barbuda, Sir Giles Bullard, had any success in convincing Gooch that it was neither expedient nor sensible to continue a battle of words with Lester Bird. Gooch by this stage was apparently threatening not to grace Antigua with his presence in the Fifth Test. It apparently never occurred to Graham in this man-made, self-inflicted, political maelstrom, that the best way to silence any critics and to gather sympathy and support for himself and his cause was to go out and score a few much needed centuries in the next two tests.

Many people failed to see why Gooch could not just focus his energies and attentions on the obvious task, and get on with the game. It had been clear right from the beginning of the tour that Gooch found very little pleasure in being in the West Indies and such vibes do have a distressing tendency to permeate a team. It is worthwhile contemplating whether lesser players of more positive attitude are not far greater and more successful assets to a side. Sadly such reflections on this tour do not apply to Graham Gooch alone.

Meanwhile, in amongst all the political posturing and 'sex, drugs, and rock'n'roll' revelations, there has been some cricket. Nothing much to write home about, admittedly, which is why most correspondents here don't, as this peripatetic cricketing nightmare gradually accumulates far more coverage in the news and feature columns than in the sports pages of the British press.

The Fourth One-day International was played in front of a capacity 25,000 Easter Monday crowd. Chanting outside the Queen's Park Oval ground was confined to the usual handful of placard-toting, anti-apartheid demonstrators. One particularly Neanderthal exponent clipped me on the shoulder and, face distorted with generic hate, denounced me as a 'white, racist, blood-sucking vampire'. I was genuinely upset and, for a few hours, unutterably miserable. I really had thought my tan was coming on rather well.

The mood inside the ground was by contrast gay and festive. Youngsters selling cool drinks, Rasta men selling peanuts, and pedlars and higglers purveying luminous red chicken, coagulated rice and peas all added to the holiday mood. I was not entirely fortunate in having a Yorkshire man of the omniscient variety sitting immediately behind me, his voice almost as loud as the fabric of his trousers. The basic problem was that he, for one, knew what the 'trouble' was.

Trouble was that there weren't enough Yorkshire men in 't

England side. Trouble was Geoffrey Boycott weren't openin' 't battin'. Trouble was these youngsters had never been down 't pits. Trouble was they didn't know what hard work was all about. Trouble was they'd never had the discipline of National Service. Trouble was they didn't know the meaning of net-practice. Trouble was they were battin' too slow. Trouble was this Tim Robinson weren't playin' enough shots. Trouble was this Tim Robinson ought to teach these West Indian blighters a lesson, accelerate 't run-rate, and cart them all over 't park.

Tim Robinson was actually playing a very diligent, extremely responsible, sheet-anchor Boycottian innings for 55. It was not exactly the cavalier, heave-ho, Beefy Botham smash-around that so empties bars and beer tents all over the cricketing world, but it was quite definitely the sort of performance many of the cricket correspondents had been demanding from the England opener since the beginning of the tour.

Our Yorkshireman was still not pleased.

'Trouble with this bloody innings . . .'

Eventually I snapped. Turning around I surveyed the little man with that Medusa-Edmonds look which has so informed my dealings with obnoxious air hostesses, shop-assistants, and wine-waiters all over the world.

'*Unus homo*,' I informed him, archly, '*Unus homo, cunctando, restituit rem.*' (With apologies to real classicists: 'One man, by blocking, saved the entire innings.')

His piggy eyes met my icy glare.

'Bloody Southerner,' he said. 'Trouble with Southerners . . .'

England failed even to make 200, despite some good swashbuckling stuff from I.T. Botham. The playing sequence on the scoreboard showed Peter Willey ahead of Botham, but quick runs were necessary at that late stage, and Beefy, if anyone, is generally the man to deliver the goods.

A hum of excitement buzzed through the crowd as the

bare-headed highlights bounced their way almost arrogantly to the crease. The West Indian crowd love a showman, and Beefy is certainly that. There is an air of hushed expectancy, whenever he approaches the wicket and, despite his poor performances thus far on the tour, everybody knows that he, above all other England cricketers, is capable of turning virtually any match around — of snatching success from the very jaws of defeat. His most acerbic detractors are often those who are disappointed that every game cannot be England versus the Australians at Headingly in 1981, and the mantle of super-stardom seems currently to be lying very heavy on those broad shoulders. If ever a man seemed in need of a straight, down-to-earth, unhyped, no-axe-to-grind, decent friend right now, it is probably Ian Botham.

A goodish slash by Botham was not enough to save England that day, since there were simply not enough runs on the board for our bowlers to have half a chance of making a contest out of it. Phil (playing in his first One-day International this trip), missed a relatively simple catch off Botham, who was genuinely and sullenly angry. A few minutes later Phil, totally atypically, misfielded a ball which continued on to the boundary. Beefy refused to pick it up. You misfielded it, his countenance and demeanour was obviously suggesting, you bloody well go and retrieve it.

At the drinks interval, I noticed David Gower specifically go over to Phil, and pat him on the shoulder, as much as to say, 'Come off it old man, it happens to everybody.' He is a man of such affable kindness, and genuine humanity, the captain. His indefatigable good temper and cheerfulness is the obverse of a coin that a lot of the band-wagon critics are billing as vapid leadership, and lack of authority. Certainly David is not in the Brian Clough mould when it comes to ordering men about. He himself is such a natural, elegant and stylish player that he has probably never had to think too hard about his own game in particular, and the entire game in general. He has been relatively lucky over the past few years in that the England team has been facing weaker

145

opposition, and therefore the much vaunted *Art of Captaincy* has never had to be called upon. His greatest sin is that he continues to treat his players as adults, and his much berated policy of 'optional nets' this tour has been predicated on the not unreasonable belief that professional cricketers are 'big boys' who should know what is best for themselves.

Unfortunately for David he is now captaining a team which looks sadly fragmented and clique-ridden after a fairly disastrous Caribbean run. Three Tests to nil down he must be *seen* to be making an effort, no matter how bad the practice facilities, no matter how fatuous the proceedings. Mike Brearley, universally acclaimed as one of England's greatest captains, was not slow to realize the value of good public relations and clever psychology. David would probably do well to take a few leaves out of his book in terms of press manipulation and image creation. Certainly when it came to 'the image', Mike Brearley would have left Saatchi and Saatchi standing; but David is of a simpler and more straightforward ilk. It is sadly beginning to look as if his *laissez-faire* attitude to the captaincy has brought the Chairman of Selectors guillotine to within centimetres of that curly, blond, insouciant head, and Peter May is making no secret of his pro-Gatting proclivities. Mike Gatting, as observers as astute as Bob Willis have not been slow to notice, has had quite a bit of spare time to lobby on his own behalf. Sporting his myriad injuries with a much lauded degree of macho-dignity he has nevertheless managed to escape with his professional reputation intact. He has yet to play in a Test Match, and has therefore not had the opportunity to dent the heroic kudos of being brutally injured in Kingston. The team has taken to calling him Cliff Richard. It is not so difficult, they feel, to be full of zest, vitality, and team ethics when far from slogging it out in the middle, you are merely on a 'Summer Holiday'.

The best, if not the only, way to while away an entire day watching cricket is to tune in to the local radio station. Tony Cozier, the only readily intelligible West Indian commentator, had unfortunately decided to take a rest from the Fourth One-day International, and had wisely remained behind in Barbados, taking a few days' well-earned break holed up in his beach house. I, for one, find it rather difficult to understand many of the other home-grown mutter-merchants, though to be fair, the locals seem to encounter no difficulties in comprehension.

We are fortunate out here to have Henry 'Blowers' Blofeld as a little light relief. In his early commentating days for the 'Beeb', Blowers would apparently stick religiously and reso-lutely to tedious details of the pitch and the game in progress. Nowadays, it is almost impossible to divert his flow into comments on such lacklustre phenomena. His is a seamless continuum of trivial leitmotifs, an art form only tangentially connected with the cricket. Pigeons, paper bags, pretty girls white parasols, butterflies, flags fluttering in the breeze, and aeroplanes are all recurrent themes in his very amusing and loquacious commentary. Cricket purists may well maintain scathingly that he is developing into a self-parody, but I on the contrary take great delight in his constant old Etonian banter.

'I say, old thing, is that an aeroplane? Any idea what sort? Yes. I can see for myself it's PamAm. I mean, what *sort*? A DC9? Oh, how splendid. Listeners, we have a DC9 flying over the ground at the moment, which seems to presage a fair degree of aerial activity this morning . . . And I say! There is a jolly pretty young lady over there in the 'Dos Santos' stand. Awfully attractive orange trouser suit . . . No, I'm sorry, it appears to be a gentleman.' (Stifled giggles, off.) 'Lord, I hope he's not listening . . .'

Of course, Blowers is missing the entire BBC commentary box gang: Trevor Bailey, Tony Lewis, Fred Trueman, Don Mosey ('The Alderman'), Brian Johnston ('Johnners') et al. I adore them all with the passion most people reserve for bad 'Soap'. Cricket, at least in *that* box, finds its rightfully mini-mal significance in the cosmic arrangement of things:

'I say, Blowers, here we have a chocolate cake kindly sent

in by Mrs Algernon Cleft-Palate-Smythe of St George's Hill,
Weybridge. Really super chocolate cake. Tony, I believe you
had a bit of luck at the golf match the other day. A dozen
pairs of tights in the raffle. What on earth will you be doing
with those?' (Dirty guffaws off-mike.) 'But this chocolate
cake really is super. And Mrs Cleft-Palate Smythe has
written us a letter . . . oh, a really wonderful letter, wanting
to know what sort of a wife is Mrs Phil Edmonds. Poor man
has been wearing the same pullover with a big brown mark
at the back — oh, and there goes Gooch, caught in the
gully — for the past four Test Matches! I say, Fred! Is that
your second slice?'

'And who have we got coming in now? Yes, the bowler's
Holding, the batsman's Willey . . ' (Apoplectic tittering,
and five minutes of broadcasting silence.)

How on earth would we be able to follow what is going on
without them?

Whilst the commentary box was really rather aimiably
jolly that day at Queen's Park Oval, the Press Box *ab
contrario* was busily psyching itself into yet more venemous
outrage. Fielding on the boundary, Ian Botham was not
exactly staving off the crowd's attentions. Multi-coloured
groupettes (small groupies, who have not yet reached the age
of puberty) not entirely discouraged in their mission, were
constantly pestering him for autographs and snap-shots. He
strolled along the boundary, his sun-hat perched jauntily
askew on his peroxide perm, did a few curtain calls, and
accepted dubious drinks. It was all fairly good-humoured
stuff, and despite the circus act he never missed a single ball,
fielded brilliantly, and stopped some certain boundaries.
The vipers in the press pit, however, were blowing telephonic
gaskets, and the captain was eventually obliged to come over
to remonstrate jovially with him, tapping him on the wrists.
Shudders from the Press Box could be felt on the Richter
scale. The very tabloids, who went into such hysterical hyperbolics in 1981 when Botham won the Ashes (and Brearley
took the credit); the very journalists who were talking about

a knighthood, a 'grace and favour' home, and all but an appropriation in the Civil List are the very same folk who now want the fallen hero keel-hauled. The press create the myth, and the press undermine the myth. The harm they do to the subjects of their oscillating favour and furore is of little concern to them. Poor Botham! Publicity is such a double-edged sword. Initially it was gratuitously foisted upon him. Latterly it has been consciously sought. Presently it is destroying him.

It is beginning to look as if future England touring teams would be well advised to dispense with the redundant luxury of an assistant manager, and to hire a roving libel lawyer instead. Professional cricketers are now extremely legalistic in their approach to the press, and perhaps are beginning to see successful libel suits as a useful adjunct to their salaries. Graham Gooch received a reputed £25,000 by way of damages for comments made about him over the South African Rebel affair.

Such libel as there putatively was fades into total insignificance compared with the unadulterated vitriol dispensed in some of the local Trinidadian papers. A leader in the *Trinidad Express* of Monday 31st March 1986, for example, began with the not entirely constructive admonition of 'Go jump in a lake, Gooch'. The piece continued in highly emotive vein about Gooch 'and his fellow Judases who claimed their pieces of silver off the backs of the South African Blacks'. All good, rabble-rousing, demagogic stuff. The author, unfortunately for the credulity of his arguments, then proceeded to exhibit his own true colours.

'There was no indication by performances that either Les Taylor or Greg Thomas should have been selected above such as Norman Cowans and David Lawrence. Their only claim to fame was their journey to the darkest side of the Dark Continent.'

These, I'm afraid, are racialist words, the words of a person who will patently never rest until the entire England team is of similar hue to himself. To allege that the T.C.C.B.

(whose infinite sagacity is at times, admittedly, a tiny bit suspect) is specifically picking players *because* they have been to South Africa is excessive even by Trinidadian standards. Rather than take offence at such arrant nonsense, Gooch should be only too pleased that the perpetrators are clearly fanatics.

'Why on earth does Goochy *mind* what this character says?' I asked Tony Brown one afternoon, addressing the looming Antigua problem. 'And, in any event, what does it matter what the *Deputy* Prime Minister of anywhere says? Who's the *Prime* Minister?'

Tony looked at me with the sardonic smile of a man who by now knows more than he ever wanted to know about West Indian politics and politicians.

'The *Prime* Minister,' said Tony, slowly unfolding the secrets of the Antiguan masonic lodge, 'The *Prime* Minister, I'm afraid, is Lester's dad.'

It took the Eton and Cambridge perspective of people like Henry Blofeld to put old Lester in his correct historic context. Blithely strutting the stage of international politics in 1986, Lester Bird was, in 1981, the West Indian Board of Control representative for the Leeward Islands. In 1981 we had, of course, 'The Jackman Affair'. The Prime Minister of Guyana, Forbes Burnham, took exception to England substitute Robin Jackman and his 'South African connections'. Forbes' case was incontrovertibly watertight: Jackman's wife was definitely South African, and Jackman was definitely connected to her. England's taciturn manager, A.C. Smith, would have no truck with such posturing. He virtually had a Dunkirk *genre* escape planned from the beaches, though sadly for the world's press this eventually proved redundant. There was even talk that Lester was (at that time) an aspiring Test commentator, and the last thing he wanted to see was his embryonic career on the broadcasting waves blown by any fool politicians. He was the first to ensure that the Antigua Test went on regardless, and that the England players were welcomed to the island with open arms.

If a week is a long time in British politics, then surely five years must be an eternity in the Caribbean variety. Lester seems to have done a complete *volte-face*. We shall have to wait and see how many people have espoused his cause when we reach Antigua.

This tour really is degenerating into an amalgam of petty politics and spurious sensationalism. The beleaguered Botham is busily issuing yet another writ, against yet another Sunday tabloid, for yet another allegation suggesting that he no longer wants to play for England. He has just been more or less obliged to part company with his agent, the flamboyant eccentric millionaire Tim Hudson, after some story appeared in *The Daily Star* alleging that Hudson at a Malibu party said something along the lines of: 'of course Botham takes drugs. Doesn't everyone?'

'Oh, God,' winced Matthew Engel, staring lugubriously into his luncheon gazpacho in the Trinidad Hilton Coffee Shop when he heard the reported Hudson gaffe. 'Now they're stabbing Botham in the *front*.'

Hudson denied the quotations. Many people were not unhappy to see the Hudson — Botham relationship broken, least of all, by press accounts, Botham's father-in-law, who apparently suggested opening celebratory bottles of champagne. It was widely felt, in cricketing circles, that Hudson had filled Ian's head with promises of mega-bucks, super-stardom and Hollywood. In the process, Botham's cricket, the one and only attribute that has made him a marketable commodity and a genuine hero, has taken a nose-dive.

For the first time in a long time, Botham's place in the Fourth Test in Trinidad was in jeopardy. It also looked very much as if Peter May had delivered a very serious, if totally negative, message to the captain: at all events, avoid a repetition of 1984; avoid another blackwash. The English team therefore played an extra batsman to the exclusion of the specialist bowler and Phil, the left-arm spinner, was twelfth man. He was not exactly pleased, but there again, neither was Richard Ellison, nor Les Taylor, who has hardly been played this tour.

It is so glaringly obvious to any casual observer with the merest smattering of common sense that this team is suffering from a highly detrimental break-down in communications. After a brilliant piece of bowling in the One-day International way back in Jamaica, Les Taylor has been left inexplicably on the side-lines. Richard Ellison, generally accepted as the best quick bowler we have, was staggered not even to make the twelve. Phil, more philosophical but equally cheesed off, surmised that England were going for a draw with 'defeatist fucking tactics' (as they are apparently called in expert professional cricketing parlance). The problem here is that nobody bothers to explain to players what is happening and why. If team meetings were used to make people comprehend the group objective, then possibly players, even non-playing players, might be more able and willing to contribute to its ultimate fulfilment. There is nothing more pernicious than disgruntled, omitted players wondering what on earth they have done *wrong*. Chances are, they haven't done anything wrong, especially not the bowlers. The trouble on this tour is that the overall balance of the side has been disrupted by the ever increasingly frenetic efforts to compensate for the shoddy batting, which the consequently omitted specialist bowlers quite obviously resent.

Well, 'the defeatist fucking tactics' were not exactly crowned with success, and the West Indies won the match by ten wickets. It seems to me, as a total *ingénue*, that if the batting does come off, then the extra batsman is redundant and you need your extra bowler to bowl the opposition out: and if the batting disintegrates, then your extra batsman is probably worth only another five or six runs in any event. Such thinking however is obviously far too simplistic amongst all these Mensa cricket minds, and so I shall keep it quite properly to myself.

The inevitable happened. Greg Thomas, our Welsh—

English fast bowler, had a nightmare match, but was unfortunately obliged to continue bowling since the captain only had three other top-class bowlers to choose from (Botham, Emburey, and Foster). Botham, perhaps for once realizing that his career as a Test cricketer — for reasons on and off the field — was on the line, exhibited a few glimmering sparks of that old Botham fire, and, as most successful bowler, collected five wickets and was second best batsman.

The best England batsman, and the most pedagogic example to the rest of the ailing team, was Worcestershire's David Smith. David is a huge man of few words; a red-head with a reputation for aggression against fast bowlers, and indeed against anyone who rouses his normally phlegmatic temper. There is a very endearing kindliness about him with respect to members of the 'weaker sex'. After some particularly raucous and generally unpleasant behaviour perpetrated by just one unstoppable member of the team on the transfer bus from Trinidad airport to the Hilton for the Second Test, David Smith apologized to me for his colleague's behaviour on behalf of the entire team. I, to tell the truth, was very touched. Phil has always said to me (and of course there is reason in what he says), that if a wife travels with the team, she must not expect any behavioural concessions to be made to accommodate her presence and I certainly never expect any. In his quiet, unfussy sort of way however, David felt sorry and embarrassed for me, and in so doing showed himself to be a gentleman of far finer sensitivities than my own dear husband.

I digress. David Smith's philosophy for success is simple. It is based on the very tenets which the West Indian pace-bowlers seem to have embraced with such devastating results. The secret is channelled hate. Off the field everybody may well be very matey, but on the field, facing guys who would gladly dislodge your cranium from the top of your spinal cord in intimidatory efforts to collect your wicket, the only answer is to match hate with hate. Observers have commented sweetly on how nice it is to see Ian Botham at the wicket, having a laugh and a jape with the godfather of his first son and his best chum, Viv Richards. 'Isn't it great to see such friendly rivalry?' they ask, so crucially missing the point. The point is that the only way to stay with the West Indians is to match fire with fire, hostility with hostility, aggression with aggression. As Australian wicket-keeper Rodney Marsh apparently once told a nervously chatting Derek Randall as he tried hopelessly to engage the impervious Antipodean in conversational banter at the crease: 'What d'you think this is? A fucking garden party?' (They really do have such a way with words, these colonials.)

There is only one winner in these Botham—Richards exchanges of wit and repartee, and it is certainly not I.T. Botham (whose concentration could be far better focused on the job in hand). Indeed, when it comes to the crunch, Viv Richards does not have the look of a jolly conversationalist when he's at the crease . . .

A lot more aggression, then, and far fewer Oscar performances it would seem is the recipe for an immediate improvement in the side. By Oscar performances, I do not, unfortunately, mean award-winning centuries. No. These performances are well-orchestrated R.A.D.A.-worthy histrionics, prize exhibitions of agony and pain, premature apologies for subsequent dismissal, or perhaps merely ostentatious complaints from the middle about the uneven bounce of the pitch. It never ceases to amaze me that a ball which hits, say, Graham Gooch or Wilf Slack on the hand seems to have an exponentially more painful effect on, for example, Ian Botham. Wilf and Graham will just take off the glove, give the hand a quick matter-of-fact, no-fuss rub, and, concentration unbroken, return to face the music. Sometimes you see them mouth the odd word of polite recrimination — 'Oh Gosh!', or 'Dear Me' can occasionally be lip-read — but obdurately, they continue with their innings.

One cannot help but wonder whether Beefy Botham on the contrary has not had one M.G.M. screen test too many. Indubitably painful though a knock on the glove must be, it is highly doubtful whether ten minutes ranting and wailing, in the best classical Greek chorus tradition, has a terribly good psychological effect on the next poor blighter padded up. According to Phil, who was absolutely incensed over such an occurrence one evening, the ham acting and vituperative complaints about the pitch and the bowling spill over into the dressing room upon dismissal, do far more than any West Indian paceman to psyche our next poor batsman out.

'I just wouldn't allow it!' said Phil dogmatically.

It is, of course, a constant source of frustration and annoyance to Phil, one of the more thinking and articulate members of the team (God knows, it isn't difficult), that he is in no position of authority to decide what is or is not allowed. At the moment, or so it would seem, anything but anything goes.

14

The world's news

Donald Carr, the Secretary of the T.C.C.B., arrived hot-foot late on Sunday 6th April, missing the end of the Fourth truncated Test, and bearing missives from Lord's. Peter May, the Chairman of Selectors, had come all the way to Barbados, presumably, as far as one could ascertain, to do very little other than carry Graham Gooch's letter back to the T.C.C.B. in London. Donald Carr was then dispatched from London to Graham Gooch in Trinidad with the T.C.C.B.'s reply. Seriously, the sooner Lord's learns about stamps the better.

Would Gooch go to Antigua? Could he be persuaded? What threats or promises could be brought to bear to convince him? Did he still have South African 'connections'? By the time these and many other Gooch-related questions could be answered, nobody gave a proverbial toss.

Dear Donald Carr. He came to Port of Spain thinking he had no more Herculean a task than to sort out Graham Gooch. He reminded me of the much harrassed Pharoah of Egypt; poor man was expecting nothing more aggravating than the odd plague of locusts to deal with when God zipped in and zapped him with 'a swift death of all the first-born'. That very Sunday's *News of the World* carried some pretty 'amazing revelations' from an ex-Miss Barbados. (That is, an 'ex' of well over a decade ago: I mean, let's face it girls, things can happen in that time. Even Liverpool Lime Street Railway Station looked good then.)

Well, ex-Miss B., Lindy Field, had some wonderfully ripping yarns to tell. Steamy nights during the Third Test in our sleepy Lemon Arbour in Barbados. Nights allegedly spent

with a *top* England cricketer (up till this point no one in the
press had admitted that there *even was* such a thing on this
tour). Nights making love in such a passionate and energetic
fashion that the bed broke. Nights so passionate that aforementioned top cricketer was unfit to play for some part of the
Test. (Incidentally I've asked England physiotherapist
Laurie Brown for a list of all those suffering from non-
specific 'groin strains' that match.) Oh, ex-Miss B. had a
wonderful field-day and by all accounts some lucky man had
had a wonderful Field-night. There were allegations of Ms
Field and companion snorting cocaine, too, unbeknown to
their dinner hosts Mick Jagger and Jerry Hall. It was all
pretty detailed, lascivious and totally damning stuff.

'Door-stepping' around the Trinidad Hilton's swimming
pool from 8.30 am to 5 pm, waiting to hear if Gooch was
going to Antigua or not, the rare copies of *News of the World*
flown in by the British Airways crew were swapping hands at
vertiginous speed.

'Two banana daiquiris and an autographed England
cricket bat for a quick butcher's,' bargained Phil with a
British Airways steward.

'Forget the bat, dearie. I'll settle for the banana daquiris,'
pouted our steward provocatively, and off he minced for his
priceless first-day, mint-condition issue.

Everybody found the whole business convulsively funny
but I, for one, found it deeply depressing. Clusters of
cricketers and pressmen swooped on the available papers
like ravenous gannets. The mirth was uncontrollable. Senior
members of the West Indian Board of Control fought hard to
contain the tears of laughter. Fortunately for them, the West
Indies has not yet reached that zenith of civilization which
engenders and promotes newspapers predicated on little else
than mammoth mammaries and the ubiquitous odysseys of
superstars' roving genitalia. Oblique reference, it is true, was
made to some character 'smokey Joe' (sic), apparently a top
West Indian cricketing superstar, whose sex and dope proclivities inevitably left our boy standing. But who was going

to haul a West Indian cricketer over the coals? The West Indians, after all, are winning . . .

People gorged themselves on every syllable of Ms Field's salacious story. As ex-Miss B. completed the thorough hatchet-job on her 'handsome sportsman' she wished, somewhat belatedly, that the whole thing could have remained 'our secret'. Having sold the tale to the *News of the World* for a substantial five-figure sum it was, of course, just bound to remain a secret. Beauty contestants, as we are all painfully aware, are not generally selected for their cerebral qualities. (If I win, I would like to travel the world and help people — oh yeah!) This one took some beating. Educational sub-normality, (and this would appear to be the only felicitous upshot from this whole sorry saga), is patently not confined to professional sportsmen alone.

Folk continued to feast their insatiable eyes, breathlessly hungry to learn who had been the lucky recipient of Ms Field's spare 'coke' and pneumatic attentions.

'He's got the most tremendous body,' she secretly confided to several million avid readers. 'He's got such charisma and a great physique.'

Phew! Everyone's relief was visibly audible. Until then, some of the more malicious minds had genuinely thought she might have been talking about I.T. Botham.

'Door-stepping' is the expression that journalists apply to hanging around and waiting for something to happen in an indefinite future: the announcement of a Royal birth, for example; the dénouement of the Iranian Embassy siege; or, for those with faith to move mountains, a consistent and intelligent selection policy from the England management team. Eight and a half hours 'door-stepping' around the pool with the press is a far from miserable experience. Donald Carr, the outgoing Secretary of the T.C.C.B. had just been flown in especially from NW8 as an extraordinary emissary for the Antigua Tourist Board. The basic idea was to convince Graham Gooch that Antigua really was a highly desirable and generally jolly good place to go, even if father and son Bird were running it. Poor Gooch was locked up incommunicado all day with D. Carr, Tony Brown, David Gower, and Steve Camacho (the Secretary of the West Indian Board of Control). Selecting a new Pope in the Vatican Conclave cannot have been more difficult a task. Every so often Tony Brown would emerge from this cricketing Curia, to report darkly that there was still no news.

As the morning progressed and the poolside bar opened, proceedings became decidedly more jolly. The interesting feature of re-reading your own diary is that you have the opportunity to notice how your opinions and assessments of people and situations change. When the ITN and BBC camera crews originally arrived in Trinidad for the Second Test — and as everyone sincerely anticipated, for a lot of political aggro — I erroneously bracketed them along with the hotch-potch phalanx of other news hounds who all joined the ill-fated tour at that juncture. Nothing could have been further from the truth, and I am genuinely sorry to have dismissed them in such an unfairly deprecating manner earlier on. In fact, the camera crews are undisputedly the best fun and least malicious newsmen covering the tour. Of course, they do not have quite the scope for subjective vitriol that newspaper correspondents do, and I remain persuaded that had circumstances allowed greater television coverage of the tests, public interest in the written word (and hence the number of barracuda pressmen out for blood), would have been commensurately less excessive.

The BBC presenter, Mark Austin, would probably win the accolade as the best-looking man on this trip, (depressingly little competition, I'm afraid), and his ITN counterpart, Jeremy Thompson, would indubitably rank as the most outrageously funny man here. His endless anecdotes about 'tired and emotional' news readers, hiccoughing their way through live TV broadcasts reduced us to tears. One such inebriated character was apparently doing relatively well, in an ominously slurred sort of way, until he arrived at a piece on the United Kingdom's National Debt. 'And now . . . (hic)

. . . we come to the United Kingdom's National Debt . . .'
(long pause). 'The United Kingdom's National Debt is . . .'
(huge sigh and deep audible breath) '. . . five million
hundreds . . . five hundreds thousand . . . five hundred and
thousand millions . . . (hic) . . . five million and hundreds
and thousands'. . . (devastatingly long silence). 'Oh, bugger
it. It's a helluva lot of money anyway.' (Swift end of
broadcast.)

Henry 'Blowers' Blofeld was also regaling us with amusing
tales, some more repeatable than others. He told us of a trip
up north to commentate on the Test Match at Headingly
during the miners' strike, when he was apparently stopped
by some callow youth of about 18 purporting to be a policeman. Tapping officiously on the windscreen, the young con-
stable ordered Blowers to wind down the window. Blowers, of
course, in his usually charming and accommodating fashion,
was quick to oblige.

'Sir,' said the infant policeman, patently disconcerted by
Blowers' be-spectacled uppercrust face, and old Etonian
blazer and cravat. 'Sir, we have reason to believe that you
could be a flying picket.'

'Really, old thing,' exclaimed Blowers in resounding
patrician dismay. 'Do I *look* like a flying picket?'

Four hours later as morning moved inexorably into lunchtime there was still no statement from Donald Carr.

'Give me four *minutes* with Donald Carr,' groaned John
Jackson of the *Daily Mirror*, an anti-establishment man after
my own heart, 'and I'd give in.'

'They'll probably give Gooch an ultimatum,' suggested
someone else. 'Either smile or you go to Antigua.'

Chris Lander of *The Sun* rang London for information on
developments here in Trinidad. Since cricketers have been
learning of their Test selection or omission from their loved
ones in England, Chris's ploy was far from unintelligent.

'Thirty-three,' shouted someone out of the blue. There was
a rustle of note-pads as the statistic was scribbled down. As
the afternoon progressed people would forget whether the

disembodied figure related to some cricketer's age, number of Test appearances, or probable I.Q.

The poolside waitress, and *the* indisputable Hilton character was Violet. Violet was an eighteen stone Carmen Miranda, always smiling, good-humoured and cheerful, but, as her one concession to general Trinidad Hilton policy, impossibly slow. Her bosom and her hips seemed to enjoy quite separate nervous systems, and wobbled merrily along in a quite autonomous and joyfully independent fashion. Seven hours after the inception of this marathon (a meeting of which E.E.C. Agricultural Ministers in their annual price fixing rounds could be justifiably proud), Chris Lander (*The Sun*) prevailed upon Violet to ring Donald Carr.

'Hello, this is Violet from the bar,' she explained. 'I want to talk to Donald.'

But Donald, who has sadly not been in Trinidad sufficiently long to appreciate who and what is of true significance, refused to comply.

By about 4 pm I was beginning to wonder whether it wasn't high time someone advised Amnesty International of poor Gooch's plight. God knows what torture they were subjecting the man to: thumbscrews, hot needles, electric shocks, a list of the England batting averages . . . Eventually he emerged with no visible signs of maltreatment. Perhaps they had managed to brain-wash him. At all events he was looking for the physio, Laurie Brown, and complaining of a fearful headache.

Finally, around five-ish, a white puff of smoke went up from the Cricketing Curia, and Senior Cardinal Donald Carr emerged with a statement.

'Annuncio vobis gaudium magnum: habemus Goochem' ('I bring you tidings of great joy: we have a Gooch'), or something more or less along those lines. Nobody would give me a copy of the actual draft. They knew I would only bitch about the spelling and punctuation.

'Yeah, yeah, great, great, Gooch is going to Antigua,' chorused the press who recognize a totally boring anti-climax when they see one. 'Swap you my golf clubs for a *News of the World*.'

One of the people no doubt pleased to hear of Gooch's final change of heart was his inseparable 'Siamese Twin', John Emburey. 'Good job Goochy isn't going home,' was the general feeling in the camp. 'Otherwise they'd have to put Embers on a life-support system.'

Donald skedaddled before anyone could ask him about Ms Field, the cost of a London—Trinidad round-trip, or the meaning of life, the universe, and everything in general.

As night drew her dusky veil over the Trinidad Hilton, cynical minds were still meditating. Were some elements of the British press actually paying dole-queue pussy to infiltrate the England Cricket team, and indeed be infiltrated by the less discerning members of it? Could this be the dawning of a new abstemious touring team morality? Is any one night screw worth the dangers of V.D., herpes, A.I.D.S. *and* the *News of the World*?

It was all too much excitement for simple souls to suffer, and so Phil and I went to the neighbouring island of Tobago for the rest day. The terminology, I do apologize, is a trifle confusing. A 'rest day' is a day on which you would have had a rest if the Test Match had gone on for a full five days instead of folding up in an ignominious three. Other days on which you have an unexpected rest are called 'optional practice days'. I'm sure you will appreciate that the distinction, although fine, is absolutely clear.

The flight to Tobago takes as little as eight minutes and as long as thirty depending on the plane. (No, don't ask me what sort.) The fare, a mere £15 return, is heavily subsidized by central government in order to encourage tourism. The island is still wonderfully under-commercialized and beautifully unspoilt. For many years the role of poor relation to Trinidad has rankled the Tobago islanders, but now that the Trinidadian economy is suffering from a sharp downturn due to plummeting oil prices, the Tobagans are decidedly perky. Some go so far as to speak of secession from the Republic of Trinidad and Tobago, though such pipe dreams seem unlikely to meet with tangible fulfilment.

The Tobagans are far more open and friendly folk than the Trinis, and we were warmly adopted by our taxi driver as soon as we arrived at the airport.

'Hello you people,' he greeted us aimiably. 'My name's Spencer.'

Phil beat me to it with the only possible corny rejoinder.

'Really. We know your brother Marks.'

Spencer gave us a quick conducted tour of the south of the island. We drove for a good two hours before another car came along and eventually overtook us.

'Dis damn island gettin' too damn crowded,' grumbled Spencer, hitting the accelerator and reaching speeds of anything up to 20 miles per hour.

Spencer's historical perspective was delightfully Caribbean; the intrinsic understanding of the general scenario more than compensated for the lack of factual detail.

'Well first der wus dee Spanish; an' den dee French come along an' fight wid dem; an' den dee English come along an' fight wid dem; an' den dee French comin' back an' fight wid dem; an' den dee English comin' back an' fight wid dem; . . . an' I doan know what all dem people findin' to fight about in dis damn island, but in dem days we is never bein' left in peace!'

Good old Spencer. I remember him fondly. Certainly our trip to Tobago made me view the West Indies with a rather less jaundiced eye. It is a shame that we do not have the opportunity to visit more of the smaller, less American-tourist oriented, proportionately friendlier Carribbean islands. Darling Matthew Engel quite wisely cleared off to French-speaking Martinique between the Barbados and Trinidad Tests, and was thoroughly impressed with the place. These French overseas territories receive vast handouts from the Central French government, and the quality of life, food, drink and hospitality is greatly superior to many

English-speaking islands. Matthew had been to investigate the Martiniquais' national pastime, cock-fighting, a sport which he found far less depressing, and marginally less lethal than the type of cricket being currently purveyed in the Caribbean. He returned from Martinique with some very good ideas, and graciously invited Phil and me to help him drink them. Two sips of a vintage Bordeaux a few mouthfuls of Roquefort and I was back in the land of Racine, imbued with that incandescent Cartesian lucidity which lesser mortals perceive as pissed.

'There is a way,' I mused, inspired, 'we *can* beat the West Indies: Gaudeloupe, Martinique, St Martin, Haiti . . .'

It is, of course, perversely far easier to get on in a country where you know for a fact that people are speaking a foreign language. In the French West Indies, for example, either you can understand the lingo, or alternatively you cannot. The room for confusion is therefore limited. Problems of comprehension arise when different cultures use exactly the same language and words to convey totally different concepts. 'No problem' in Trinidad, for example, means 'what you have just requested is totally out of the question, and indeed I have no intention of doing anything about it anyway'. 'Soon come', anywhere in the Caribbean generally means 'whatever you have requested will arrive within the next few days'. It is such a dangerously imperfect mode of communication, language.

Again, not a soul was sorry to be leaving Trinidad. The manager, Tony Brown, and Ian Botham left one day early in order to join their wives who had flown out together to Antigua. I took the precaution of trying to pay our Hilton bill a day early, since precedent had demonstrated clearly that this was just marginally less difficult than rescheduling the entire Mexican External Trade Deficit. The bill, as is ever the case nowadays, was in no way consumer friendly. Unexplained and inexplicable figures, codes, symbols and hieroglyphics spewed out of the Hilton computer: the data-based outpourings of some terminally faulty anode.

'Look here,' I pointed out. 'There is no telephone charge here and I've made at least five intercontinental phone-calls.'

The man at the cash desk was used to argumentative guests.

'No you haven't,' he replied.

'Yes, I have,' I insisted.

'Oh, no you haven't,' he maintained unmoved.

'Oh, yes I have,' I countered unperturbed.

'Oh, no you haven't . . .'

We were oscillating between poor farce and bad pantomime. I finally gave that one up as lost.

'On the contrary,' I returned to the fray, 'you've charged me for a whole host of breakfasts I've never had.'

'Oh, no we haven't.'

'Oh, yes you have.'

'Oh, no we haven't.'

I'd had enough, and meekly proffered the relevant piece of plastic fantastic, its code-number extrusions by now worn flush with the surface.

'Hotel's busy today,' I remarked to pass the time.

'Oh, no . . .'

Yes, we were all well pleased to be on our way to Antigua.

15

Captain, the ship has sunk

Nobody knew what to expect at Antigua airport. After all the political posturing of the Deputy Prime Minister, Lester Bird, it was not entirely unreasonable to expect a massive anti-apartheid demonstration.

'Don't be stupid,' snapped Phil, in that disarmingly endearing way he always allays my deepest fears and upsets. 'All these blighters want to see is another blackwash.'

Phil is getting bored with being right this tour. Sure enough, there were a mere eight demonstrators waiting for us by the transfer bus. It is distressing to note that less and less effort is going into these affairs, and I honestly do believe that the Students' Union at the University of the West Indies has reduced them to 'Optional Demos'; a defeatist attitude is definitely permeating the weary chants.

There does not appear to be the slightest indication of any leadership or discipline. Attire is sloppy. There is not a single character who seems to be willing just to stay there and to battle it out in the sun for a few hours: no, a few quick airy-fairy wafts, a token gesture, and off. Some actually look as if they have been up all night drinking too heavily. Others are passing around some 'badly packed cigar' in a laid-back, feeling-no-pain, catatonic trance sort of way. I am, of course, still talking about the demonstrators.

It seems strange to recollect that the major problem at the beginning of this tour was potential headaches with anti-apartheid activists. As the tour has progressed such minor niggles have been relegated to the status of a burst water pipe prior to a full-scale nuclear explosion. The placards now rank no better than beta-minus for artistic content, and delta for technical merit. 'Racists, go home' was a rather lack-lustre attempt at opening the demonstrating, and any well-trained, fit and even medium-pace eye could run straight through the middle-order, wishy-washy attempts of 'Go away' and 'We don't want you here'. Honestly, after this tour, the Students' Union must do the right thing, and conduct a public inquiry into the disintegration of what originally, on paper, looked like one of the best placard-toting line-ups in the world.

The England Cricket Team's anti-apartheid slogans are in a different league. They are, of course, the subject of constant practice, and are rehearsed and rehearsed until the timing is perfect. Any minor problems of technique are assiduously ironed out, and, as an indication of true professionalism, video recordings of performances are even being mooted.

'Go Home,' shout the West Indians, monotonously.

'Gooch, the brute, took the loot,' counter the England cricket team, with world-class attention to assonance, rhyme and scansion. There is just no contest. Even making concessions for the uneven pace and bounce of the bus, England's vast superiority with the pithy slogan and the rhyming couplet is indisputable.

We arrived at the hotel to a flurry of inactivity. The rooms were not ready, and even when they were, they didn't contain any phones. The reception sported the grand total of three telephone lines for a press corps which now boasts *seven* correspondents for every England cricketer. At 11.30 am the dining room was shut for breakfast and not yet open for lunch. What do you mean, there's no coffee shop? What on earth do you expect for a mere US$200 a night? You're the sort that would be demanding airconditioning and a television set! Honestly, I do strongly recommend that before anyone books their holiday trip of a lifetime to Antigua, *please* consult the *Spanish* Tourist and Information Board.

This hotel is just the sort of joint that makes my blood boil: more expensive than Claridge's, provocatively slow service, and the general attitude sullen and resentful. To add insult to injury, prices were inexplicably and exorbitantly expensive, and the pretension ridiculous. The dining room, for example, was a fairly airless corrugated iron extension, and birds riddled with who-knows-what contagious diseases were busily pecking at crumbs left on the tables. The food was what a fussy Frenchman could conceivably depict as 'infect'. House rules demanded, however, that gentlemen must wear jackets for dinner. It was tantamount to insisting that ladies wear a tiara to shop at Portobello Road street market (where incidentally the food is exponentially better).

I subsequently read a piece in a British Sunday newspaper gossip column, penned by yet another of those wearisome creatures who have not been within 5,000 miles of the tour, and yet feel they have the god-given right to jump on the inquisitional band-wagon and have a good go at the England team. Well, this particular columnist had apparently *heard* from a friend of an acquaintance of a woman who used to baby-sit for the budgerigar of a third-cousin-twice-removed-by-a-previous-divorce of a man who used to go to Tupperware parties with an American lady who was staying here, that she was absolutely scandalized by the fact that the England cricketers used to turn up for dinner in the dining room *without* jackets. Difficult, indeed dangerous though it is to argue with such patently incontrovertible and impeccable sources, I am afraid that for once I must champion the England players' cause. Brilliant they may not all be, but at US$30 a throw for the sort of stuff that would make even British Rail habitués shudder, not one of them was actually dumb enough to eat dinner in the dining room.

So incensed was I by the sheer pretentiousness of the place that I was finally moved to verse, the results of which I consigned to the manager:

'For crêpes bien flambées
I'll dress as you say.
But

For cold rice and peas
I'll dress as I please.'

I was not at all surprised to receive no reply.

The hotel is now absolutely swarming with press. Regular cricket correspondents are totally outnumbered by news hounds, many of whom have been flown in from Florida and New York in ever exaggerated efforts to catch even the vaguest whiff of scandal.

Lindsay Lamb and Alison Downton, both of whom had travelled directly to Antigua from Barbados, were rather put out when they booked into the hotel a few hours before the rest of us arrived. They were accosted by some dirty old hack of the flashermack variety, who told them that they were in for 'a good time': the England Cricket Team, he apprised them, was about to arrive and they would be 'all right for the week'. The rest of the press loved this rampant 'sex-machine' story, naturally, and dutifully published it as yet another nail in the England touring coffin. What nobody bothered to relate was the codicil. 'If you don't manage to score with the team,' he continued to explain, 'there's always plenty of pressmen around as consolation prizes'. Our hack in the mack at least knew his press boys. As for the cricketers, he had never seen them before in his life . . .

A letter had arrived from my brother, Brendan, the eye surgeon in Kingston. He had noticed an advertisement in the 'situations vacant' columns of a medical magazine which purported to be that of a private maternity clinic in Kingston, but which was obviously a covert and rather desperate appeal from Lord's:

'Come and work in a sunny climate:
Free white uniform provided:
No previous specialist experience necessary:
Guaranteed three day week.'

Dear Brendan. It hardly seemed three months ago that I was flying out to see him and all my friends at the University of the West Indies. Waltzing around the Caribbean in this strange England touring bubble, we seem to have lost all touch with reality: with *real* people, *real* problems, and *real* life.

On the contrary, life on this final leg of the West Indies tour has moved into the surreal; photographers popping up from behind coconut trees to take subsequently damning pictures of any England cricketer who picks up a glass or so much as speaks (Shock! Horror!) to a 'woman'; gossip columnists who know so much about what's going on that they still think Wilf Slack is the cocktail waiter; a praetorian guard of *Sun* newspaper minders, remorselessly 'protecting' the happily-reunited Botham couple from the predatory advances of any other newsmen. The scenes are pure undiluted Kafka, although the conversation naturally remains resolutely Pinter.

A few observers are beginning to perceive Botham's loyalty to one newspaper, *The Sun*, as deleterious to the team. Far more are beginning to see it as highly damaging to Botham himself. For a reputed £40,000 a year, *The Sun* is entitled to Beefy's 'exclusive' services, which means that other newspapers find it difficult, indeed well nigh impossible, to get hold of Botham quotes, stories and pictures. *The Sun*'s new cricket correspondent, Chris Lander, who 'ghost-writes' the Botham column is Ian's friend, mentor, and close companion on tour. Lander, prior to his new appointment, accompanied Botham on the well-publicized charity walk from John o'Groats to Land's End, and after that the die was inexorably cast. The former *Sun* correspondent, Steve Whiting, was relieved of his cricketing post, and the job went conveniently to Lander. Whiting's wife, who by her own account has been a drug user, has made a sworn-affidavit to the *News of the World* about Botham's private life. It is quite extraordinary, the amount of money being made available by Fleet Street for discrediting stories about Ian Botham.

One of the major problems would now seem to be that this cricket tour has degenerated into the battlefield of a tabloid circulation war. On the one hand, we have the *News of the World* maintaining that Botham is the worst thing since a saturated fat diet, and on the other hand we have *The Sun* stalwartly insisting that he is the very best thing since sliced wholemeal bread. Interestingly, these two publications are 'sister-papers' — from the same stable. One cannot help wondering whether they are 'creating' news where there isn't any, in order to increase sales. At any event, perhaps somewhere between the two story-line extremes lies the real truth of the man.

The current danger is that both the great British public, and indeed the not-so-great England cricketers are beginning to confuse media coverage with true significance. Constant attention is often correlated to real importance. Youngsters bred on television, public relations, meretricious glamour, and falling intellectual and moral standards have a distressing tendency to deify pop-stars and sportsmen, not doctors, nurses or missionaries. That is, and has always been, inevitable. The idols however, especially in the erstwhile clean-cut, 'play up, play up, and play the game' arena of cricket must understand that they have a terrible responsibility to their fans and must not, on any account, be found to have the proverbial feet of clay. God knows what damage is being done to teenagers' minds, beliefs and aspirations by the sensational allegations emerging from this tour.

The first evening in Antigua the team was invited by the sponsors, Cable and Wireless, to a cocktail party at the exclusive and prestigious St James' Club on the other side of the island. Yes, I suppose I *could* find out for the pernickety geographers amongst you whether 'the other side' means north, south, west or east, but by this stage of the tour, quite frankly, who cares about *facts*?

The multi-millionaire owner of the St James' Club, Peter de Savary, was sadly nowhere in evidence, but generously the facilities of the Club were extended to the entire team, a gesture which, *de facto*, put paid to any claims of exclusivity and prestige. The club, nevertheless, does remain the

Caribbean hideaway for many of the rich and famous and for prices as low as US$500 a night, for example, you too can rub knees with the likes of Terry Wogan, or so at least one of the sponsors informed me. Nowadays it's difficult to believe *anything* that *anybody* says.

Most of the genuine 'cricket correspondents' (a virtually extinct breed by this juncture) had boycotted the party. Cable and Wireless had specifically omitted to invite two of the most outstanding genuine cricket correspondents, Matthew Engel and Robin Marlar, because these two writers allegedly omit to mention the names of any sponsors in their copy. Most of the others C.C.'s were outraged, but sadly sponsors these days insist on their pound of flesh. All of the newshounds who were, on the contrary, invited to the party, have understood that freebie pencils and notepads must be repaid in kind. From now on we shall no doubt read about the Cable and Wireless *sponsored* 'Shock, horror, phew what a scorcher' torrid nights with ex-Miss First Flushing Lavatory, 1937. It is becoming increasingly impossible to treat this peripatetic circus as anything other than a very bad joke.

Phil was again furious not to be selected for this Test, and was frustratingly relegated to drinks-trolley manager. He is, I'm afraid, beginning to sound like a latter-day Fred Truman.

'It's like a bloody kindergarten!' he complained disgusted. 'In my day we used to bowl 50 overs at a stretch, and no arsing around. Nowadays these guys bowl two overs, and then they have to have a drink and a couple of aspirins. It started with Both, and now you've got Foster at it . . . (dark muttering) . . .'

I went, with holidaying friends, to watch England bat on the third day of the Test. I had followed the previous two days' play on the radio, and proceedings seemed to have developed into the hyperbolical lunacy of the Tom Sharpe novels the boys are all so fond of reading.

'My car, my car,' wailed one Antiguan commentator, as

Botham was brought back into the attack. It had been suggested that the way Beefy was bowling, David Gower would be better off with seven men on the boundary and two in the car park. Botham was within two wickets of Australian fast-bowler Dennis Lillee's 355 Test wicket record, and despite being carted all over the park looked as if he might start insisting to bowl from both ends. Foster and Ellison were also given some fairly rough treatment as the West Indian score moved unstoppably on. By the second day's post-luncheon session, the commentators were becoming more acerbically critical of the England captain's 'make Both a Hero at all costs' strategy. The team's most successful bowler, off-spinner John Emburey, the only man with half a chance of staying the onslaught, was unaccountably called upon to bowl but a few overs in the afternoon.

'Please, Sir, may I have my ball back,' seemed to be the captain's approach every time he had the temerity to snatch it from Botham's greedy grasp. Commentators were not slow to point out that at four Tests to nil down, and with 474 West Indian runs on the board in the fifth, personal performance and individual statistics should not have been given precedence over best possible team tactics . . .

'Captain, the ship is sinking', raged the ear-splitting Calypso rhythms from the shed-sized speakers located in the 'Double-Decker' Stand at the Antigua Recreation Grounds. The song, written and performed by calypso king, Gypsy, had originally been penned as satirical commentary on the Prime Minister of Trinidad, George Chambers, and the parlous state of his country's finances. It has sadly become disturbingly more apposite for the beleaguered David Gower, and the shambolic state of his country's cricket.

'Oh, dear, what can the matter be?' and 'London Bridge is falling down', the good-natured crowd had sung in Trinidad.

'Captain, the ship is sinking,' they chanted in Antigua. 'Captain, tell us what to do!'

Blowers was in fine fettle in the commentary box: 'Yes, and it's a glorious day here today at the Antigua Recreation

Grounds, even better than yesterday, although yesterday was absolutely perfect.' I wonder if anyone will ever collate a collection of 'Blowers-Balls'?

The other wives and assimilated consorts had been accommodated in relative splendour in the 'Viv Richards V.I.P. Stand', but unaccountably Ms Edmonds' complimentary tickets entitled her to nothing more luxurious than a hard wooden bench in the Double-Decker Stand with the hoipolloi. The place was a potential inferno, and would certainly never have passed muster with the G.L.C. (May they rest in peace, together with all their 'Equal-rights-for-gay-whales-one-parent-lesbian-family-Friends-of-the-Earth-anti-nuclear fellow travellers.)

Empty drinks cans were constantly being rolled down the corrugated tin roof, creating the most thunderous racket. Rollicking men pranced around with free-style sandwich boards, advertising 'Stuff Shellfish an Dumplin' (sic) and enjoining us to go to a neighbouring 'nite-club' — in fact the local brothel. The atmosphere was terrific. Non-stop reggae music preceded play. At the beginning of this tour I used to find reggae music a drearily monotonous dirge, a cross between bored and querulous children doggedly reciting their 'times-tables' and uncompromisingly bad Gregorian plain chant. I'd purveyed enough of both way back in the convent. Gradually, however, the atavistic rhythms get to even the most impervious of audiences, and you find yourself involuntarily just movin' to the music. Yeah, man.

Before the match started, the West Indians did quite a bit of flashy fielding practice, presumably so that Viv Richards could show his home crowd what an awfully clever little person he possibly is. The West Indians' physiotherapist, Australian Dennis Waight, sat all alone in the middle of the field and did the 'Jane Fonda Workout for Terminally Ostentatious Show-offs'. The England team was nowhere to be seen. Presumably they were in the dressing room doing group therapy: knitting, tatting, macramé.

From the penitential wooden benches in the Double-

Decker Stand, there is an unhampered view of the parish church to the right, and the local prison to the left. In between the church and the prison stands the casino. Could there, somewhere, be a moral in all this?

'Baby, you're so excitable', pounded *Amazulu* over the loud speakers as the England opening pair walked slowly to the crease. Surely, this could not be intended for, of all people, Wilf Slack? Nor yet indeed for the laconic Graham Gooch. 'I hang on 'cos I can't let go.' No, it clearly wasn't dedicated to any of *our* boys.

The most striking characteristic of any Caribbean crowd is the brightness and gaiety of the colours. It was Sunday, and many people had obviously come straight from church, still be-decked in their Sabbath finery, to worship at the *other* West Indian shrine, the cricket ground. Another noteworthy phenomenon is that ladies, even middle-aged and elderly ladies, have no qualms about coming along to the cricket on their own, and are patently, even frighteningly, well informed on proceedings. With television sets here the privilege of only the affluent few, children are brought up watching the national sport live, and osmotically assimilating folk-wisdom from all the surrounding spectators.

'That one seemed to turn a bit,' remarked some upper-crust old English gent, as West Indian off-spinner, Harper, was brought unusually into the attack.

'Pitched leg, turned off,' corrected some aimiable old West Indian dame, well into her seventies. It was as if he'd got the words of the Lord's prayer wrong.

The crowd gave a rousing cheer as 'King Dyall' took his bow in the Double-Decker stand. This frail, aged, West Indian gent is a familiar figure both at the Barbados and Antigua cricket grounds, his outrageously garish garb creating a stir whenever he appears. Today he looked resplendent in a salmon pink suit, with off-orange trimmings. By way of adornment he was sporting a mottled yellow and orange carnation in his buttonhole, canary yellow bow-tie, startlingly white gloves, thick black spectacles, a brown cane, and a pinky-mauve trilby hat. He looked about as co-ordinated as the England team's fielding the previous day.

After a few overs Viv Richards, the West Indian captain, started acting up again. He wanted yet another ball. Twenty minutes play had been lost during the Saturday afternoon's session, because Viv had wanted another ball even then. Nobody could actually establish what was ever wrong with the original ball, apart from the fact that England had managed to accumulate all of 40 runs on the board, and the West Indians had still not claimed a single wicket. I've heard people talk about Viv Richards being 'genial'. It must be that old problem of the same words conveying totally different concepts in different cultures. To the casual observer, his demeanour appears to be demonically arrogant in victory, and truculently petulant at the slightest hint of adversity, though God knows on this tour, the West Indian captain has had little enough experience of that. Whatever the critics may say about their current whipping-boy, David Gower, he is every inch the perfect English gent in success and failure alike. On the contrary, after the one match that the West Indians *lost* (remember that, the Second One-day International in Trinidad?), Viv Richards was moodily unavailable for comment. In my book at least, that is just not the behaviour of a great man or a great captain.

Back to the balls. The original ball had been a 'Duke'. Possible replacement balls, of a similar number of overs' wear, were only available in 'Stuart Surridge'. No, said the West Indian Captain. He absolutely wanted a Duke. (Well, I mean, darling, don't we all?) Indeed the bottom line, insisted Robespierre Richards, would be a slightly roughed up new Duke, although this would obviously be an immense advantage to the West Indian pace bowlers. After much acrimonious debate, the umpires, wisely, refused.

Men who turn ugly when slightly crossed are not true superstars, and certainly not the figures for impressionable young fans to emulate. Even Phil, who has seen rather more cricket than I have, which explains, incidentally, why his brains are proportionally more addled, admitted that he had never seen such an appalling display of petulance, and such needless confrontation with the umpires. Of course, adulation of Viv Richards in his home island of Antigua has reached such blasphemous levels that he can do no wrong. The double standards of cricketing establishments all over the world were again quite startlingly evident. My own husband was dropped from Test Cricket for two years over an *alleged* sledging incident with an Indian batsman, but 'superstars', both black and white, are constantly allowed to get away with murder. Viv, it is true, at the end of the match, when the 5—0 Test blackwash was in the bag, had the grace to apologize to the umpires for his outbursts. Graciousness in success, however, is not a particularly outstanding attribute. Neither is boorish behaviour. Nor manic megalomania. One genuinely begins to wonder whether there could be something wrong with the air in Somerset.

The 'balls-debate' was swiftly followed by another major incident. The groundsmen were called on to the pitch to deal with (opinions in the commentary box were sharply divided), what looked like a cow pat, but could equally well have been a doggy turd. It was all fairly gripping stuff.

Meanwhile, in the real world, American F-111s were setting off from English shores to bomb Libya . . .

Gooch and Slack batted well but the inexorable England domino effect phenomenon soon followed. The West Indians' second innings was hell-bent on scoring quick runs. Viv Richards smacked an amazing century in the fewest balls ever — 56. 'To watch the West Indians captain laying into the demoralized English bowlers,' said Tony Cozier from the commentary box, 'is like watching Martina Navratilova playing little Orphan Annie!' At 100, Richards went down on his haunches and heroically accepted the thunderous applause of his faithful worshippers. He brushed either the tears or the sweat from his eyes, and the adoring crowd went hysterical. It was such a shame I had witnessed the man's previous behaviour. I so much wanted to feel impressed.

The rest is history. For the final day of the Test, the Antiguan Government declared a national holiday so that everyone could watch England's ultimate humiliation. How this squared with the Deputy Prime Minister's injunctions to boycott the cricket is another of those Caribbean political conundrums I have yet to fathom. Gower played a captain's innings, but failed to save the match. I believe the verbal abuse that he and Downton received from Richards for their last-ditch efforts to save the game by time-wasting was choice, even by professional cricketing standards. Whatever, I ask myself, happened to that game they used to play at Cambridge?

The England team was not quite so irretrievably crumpled, nor indeed so unconsolably devasted as many people would like to imagine after their dreadful drubbing. Many, perhaps too many, players feel they have a virtual sinecure in the team. They hope they should have a relatively easy ride in the 1986 summer against the Indians and the New Zealanders, and with a winning Test team place secure their earnings will not suffer. Safely ensconced back in Lord's after his trip to Barbados, the Chairman of Selectors Peter May made ominous rumblings about 'heads rolling'. Last time there was the equally disastrous 1983—84 tour to Pakistan and New Zealand — a tour similarly hall-marked by lack of discipline and shocking behaviour all rolled together with some pretty juicy sex and dope allegations — the rolling heads were not that conspicuous. The captain of *that* ill-fated England team, Bob Willis, was made assistant manager of *this* one, and the manager of aforementioned frollicking fiasco, Doug Insole, was promoted to Chairman of the Cricket Committee of the Test and County Cricket Board, indisputably the most prestigious and influential position at Lord's. At that sort of rate neither Tony Brown nor David Gower should lose any sleep. Life peerages are probably the least they can expect.

For some days now players have been making their final departure arrangements, determined to arrive home in

England looking ship-shape and Bristol-fashion.

'Do you cut hair?' asked Greg Thomas one morning in those melodic Welsh, 'how could you ever say no' tones.

'Well I used to cut Phil's,' I was obliged to admit shame-facedly, 'and look what happened to him!'

We watched the 'Bald Eagle' (as Botham has nicknamed him) emerging from his early morning swim, the sunshine reflecting and refracting merrily off droplets dripping from his no longer excessively hirsute head. Poor darling. I have had to stop him wasting my extremely expensive pH-balanced Redken shampoo. At this stage, let's face it, a can of Pledge and a duster will do.

Our final day in Paradise was probably just one too many. Wrapped in a towel under a coconut palm, I lay shivering from the shock of a jelly-fish sting which encircled my entire waist. The wretched, formless, ectoplasmic beastie had nabbed me whilst swimming, and the most excruciating sensation of branding irons immediately ensued.

'Stop making a fuss,' said Phil. 'It'll go away in a couple of days.' Greg 'Blodwen' Thomas was somewhat more sympathetic than my own dear husband, and spoke in a disconcertingly knowledgeable lilting fashion about the 'poison seeping into your central nervous system'. Inevitably and immediately, my central nervous system began shaking, even more nervously, and I retired even further under the tree.

As I hugged my throbbing scarlet torso, and scratched the ranges of mosquito bites all over my legs which were pulsating gaily in unison like some prickly, pink Pyrenees, it occurred to me that you really can have too much of a good thing. Suddenly, a 20 pound coconut came crashing down from my protective palm tree, missing the notorious Edmonds' grey matter by mere inches, and smashing a nearby bottle of Aloe sun-tan oil into the tiniest of smithereens.

The combination of gravitational pull, and ubiquitous coconuts has turned the hotel's garden into an aerial mine-field. Only yesterday, another plummeting missile just missed a *News of the World* correspondent, almost braining him, or at least, almost expelling what was encapsulated in his head. The entire team was, of course, suitably distressed.

'Just another inch,' said eye-witness Phil . . . It's a good job, I mused philosophically to myself, that Sir Isaac Newton wasn't born in Antigua.

On our last night in Antigua the BBC and ITN camera crews threw a farewell beach party for the team at the epony-mous 'Shorty's'. Each crew generously donated a couple of hundred pounds for the purchase of comestibles, and more importantly, drinkables, and asked participating members of the press for a £5 contribution as a token gesture to defray expenditure.

Pressmen, as every British High Commissioner or Gover-nor General on this tour would probably bear me out elo-quently, are always the first to come and the last to leave any 'freebie' cocktail party. For this particular gathering, how-ever, the thought of parting with a fiver so shocked and horri-fied the majority of our egregious press corps that only a few of them showed up.

And after signing a sworn affidavit, and accepting an undisclosed five figure sum, yes folks, I, Miss Ex-French 'O' Level 1978, am going to name those I saw:

Dominic Allen (*London Broadcasting Company*)
Ted Corbett (*The Daily Star*)
Matthew Engel (*The Guardian*)
Chris Lander (*The Sun*)
John Jackson (*Daily Mirror*)
Graham Otway (*Today*), and
Peter Smith (*Daily Mail*)

Some, presumably, spent the evening poring over their expenses — along with the rest of their copy.

Departure day was not exactly funereal, though there were a few bleary eyes as the team began its two-leg trip back to London, leaving Ian Botham behind for a quiet, restful week alone with his wife and the odd *Sun* reporter. First, we flew from Antigua to Kingston, a three-hour flight spent playing silly crossword puzzle games and filling in our customs and immigration forms. A few of the press were coming back with us. Matthew Engel, in particular, was intent on filling in his forms with a degree of irrelevant veracity that was highly liable to have him thrown in the slammer yet again.

'Passport number.' That was at least one question we could all answer, without undue mental stress.

'Type of passport.'

'Large, blue, rectangular,' began Matthew.

'Are you (*or any member of your party*) carrying illegal drugs?'

'I'm afraid I'll have to take the Fifth Amendment on that one,' he continued, punctiliously. I swear that boy has not been the same since they locked him up with Geoffrey Boycott.

The baggage took ages to arrive at Kingston, and we hung around for at least an hour in the Arrivals Hall playing 'Optional Practice' with an erratic red, bouncy ball.

'Too little, too late,' growled one ancient be-hacking-jacketed old gent recently arrived from London. He was, one supposes, perfectly right.

We spent the intervening time between our arrival in Kingston, and our subsequent departure to London, at 'Captain Morgan's Harbour' for a final swim in the Caribbean sunshine. Everyone was pleased to be going home, and these last few frustrating hours lay heavily on our hands.

The return British Airways flight was uncomfortably full, the team travelling home in the relative comfort of Club Class, and the Ginger Group in steerage. It was a far cry from my First Class voyage out, with hopes so high and enthusiasm so irrepressible. Nevertheless, the unflaggingly cheerful Allan Lamb; the master purveyor of edibles and drinkables, Mike Gatting; and even the generally fun-restraining spectre at the feast, Phil Edmonds, kept us supplied with plentiful quantities of the old bubbly stuff.

'I'm afraid I'm going to have to charge you corkage on that,' one mincing little British Airways steward suggested menacingly to Lindsay Lamb. He didn't, I can assure you, make the same suggestion twice.

We arrived to a bitterly cold, grey day in London, and were ushered into Heathrow Airport's brand new Terminal Four building. The England team's baggage took two and a half hours to arrive, as each and every item was not only checked by trained sniffer dogs, but also carefully hand-searched. For the first time I was struck by the full ignominious enormity of what had happened. England cricketers, once considered the country's sporting diplomats, the glorious game's roving ambassadors, were now relegated to the status of international dope-pedlars.

16

Epilogue

'When you leave the Customs hall,' ordered the natty little British Airways Public Relations man, 'could you all please try to exit together — for the photographers, you understand. Girls out of the way please, we don't want you in. Team, if you could just walk slowly, stop and smile, walk slowly, stop and smile, that would be very nice.'

'Why don't you just ask them to do the bloody Echternach Procession,' suggested a rather cold, and jet-lagged Mrs Edmonds, who had not personally benefited from the sumptuous perks of a British Airways Club Class trip. 'You know, three steps forward, two steps back.'

'No, I don't think that will be necessary,' said the P.R. man in all seriousness. 'Just the occasional pause.'

Three hours after landing, with Customs formalities finally complete, not a single player 'occasionally paused', even to draw breath. The captain and the manager, however, were press-ganged into the usual post-mortem, and must by now be realizing how the Dutch Protestants felt when the Duke of Alba moved in. However the Grand Inquisition, that possible inquiry mooted at Lord's has, so they tell us, been temporarily shelved. Shame! A T.C.C.B.-Torquemada is just what is currently needed.

Phil was stopped and could not help himself being cajoled into a television interview. What did he think about the controversy brewing over players writing for newspapers? Phil, who has a regular cricket column in *Today* (and is, incidentally, the only current England cricketer who actually writes his own column, as opposed to putting his name to a load of ghost-written stuff), responded diplomatically that he thought his scribblings were constructive and useful. (Well, he *would*, wouldn't he?)

As usual, however, everyone is so wide of the mark. Cricketers *writing* for papers is not the real problem. It is papers virtually *owning* and manipulating players that is, on the contrary, so terribly dangerous. Players who are being used as pawns in that great Fleet Street — Wapping circulation chess-game are inadvertent liabilities to themselves, and ultimately to the status of the sport. This, unfortunately, would appear to be the petard by which the bamboozled Botham is currently being hoisted.

At the taxi rank, two burly Customs and Excise men were arresting a drug-smuggler. The miscreant appeared to be a woman and black, but it was still just as well that the British press were not in attendance. A drug-smuggling England cricketer in Caribbean drag would have made such a suitable Parthian piece.

We arrived home and were happy for once to find the house unburgled. More or less everything has already been nicked: the silver, the stereo and video equipment, the oriental rugs, Phil's trophies, my pictures. I do believe the local larcenists would break in now and leave us food parcels. 'Poor Edmondses', they are probably saying down at the pub, 'they don't have two candelabras to rub together'.

It was odd, after three months of team roving and hotel living, to be home again alone with Phil. The cheese plant in my bathroom had not survived the winter, which left me with no one to talk to except him. It was late afternoon. We were too weary to unpack, we weren't hungry, and there was nothing on the television besides snooker.

'Honey, why don't you come upstairs to the bedroom,' encouraged Phil suggestively from under the connubial duvet. 'We can fill in our Income Tax returns . . .'

Such erstwhile bureaucratic nightmares are now a piece of fiscal cake, thanks to the 'Advanced Engel Form Filling Technique':

'How much do you earn?'

'Not enough.'

'How much do you spend?'

'About twice that amount.'

At this rate Matthew won't be the only one with fun tales to tell from the slammer.

The Sunday papers made fairly depressing reading. In the sensational league, there were more, by now boring, sex and heroin allegations about the 1983—84 tour to Pakistan and New Zealand. (As if there was not enough to be said about *this* tour!) At a more mundane level, there was the usual round of cavilling: England team outbowled, outbatted, and outfielded. Fair comment from eye witnesses. Somewhat less fair comment, however, was that of the 5,000 mile remote eye-witness columnist promulgating yet more trash about the England team's sartorial displays. Even when it came to dress, apparently, the West Indians were smarter than us. I suppose next they'll be saying that the West Indians brush their teeth more often and clean behind their ears more assiduously. Such is the level of this band-wagon criticism.

An interesting Freudian slip! I seem to have stopped talking about the England team in terms of a third person plural 'they', and started talking in terms of a first person plural 'we' and 'us'. Indeed, after three months living with these characters, it is difficult not to develop an affectionate association and, barring a couple of exceptions, I would be hard pushed to say that I have not become almost fraternally fond of them all.

Love them or hate them, nevertheless, this tour is being billed as the most disastrous ever, and scapegoats are being desperately sought. Many observers (even the usually sympathetic editor of *The Cricketer* magazine, Christopher Martin-Jenkins), have suggested that the approach of two of the most senior players, Graham Gooch and Ian Botham, may have been counter-productive. A 'mere' £10,000 for a gruelling West Indian tour after record Benefits and unprecedented sponsorship deals, may not seem that attractive a proposition. Perhaps it might not therefore be too unreasonable to suggest that cricketers whose ambitious edge has been temporarily blunted by an apparent disillusionment with touring should be given either a voluntary or compulsory rest from it.

The England captaincy, too, is inevitably up for grabs. The pro-Gatting faction make much of the 'totally unplayable ball' to which he fell for one run in the second innings of his one and only Test Match in Antigua. Meanwhile, the cricketing tricoteuses watch gleefully as that selectorial guillotine seems to edge perceptibly closer to poor Gower's curly, blond head. Despite emerging as England's most successful batsman, he had fallen markedly out of favour. His captain's innings for 90, as a final last-ditch stand against the inevitable blackwash, looked to executioners, both 'awkward' and 'fragile'. Better, it would seem, to look bullish for one than fragile for a ton.

Robin Marlar, who apart from being cricket correspondent for *The Sunday Times* is consultant to a firm of 'Head-Hunters', is even suggesting the dreaded Phil Edmonds as captain. As a 'head-hunter', Robin reckons he recognizes the qualities of natural authority and leadership when he sees them. The T.C.C.B. sadly is not yet a sufficiently professional outfit to hire him!

The concept of a cricket 'supremo', a football manager-type figure is even being mooted: someone who would take complete control of players' activities on and off the field. It is all so much ado about nothing. What's in a name? All that is really necessary is one person strong enough and bright enough both to command his players' loyalty and respect and to deal intelligently with the press. The title of such a person *should* be captain, though when I say that the captain should be a 'rounded personality', I do not *necessarily* mean Mike Gatting.

Enough of all that! Whoever gets the job will have a relatively easy ride for some time to come. Mike Brearley, supposedly the greatest England captain ever, certainly *did* know a thing or two about the subtle 'Art of Captaincy'.

Lesson Number One which he might have suggested would be to never lead a team to the West Indies!

It is not for me to opine about the state of West Indian pitches and practice facilities, nor indeed about the rights and wrongs of constant intimidatory bowling. Ideas about drawing lines half-way across the pitch seem a trifle excessive and, for what it's worth, Phil believes that fast bowlers must be allowed to bowl as they will, *provided* the pitches are true. Fears about the gradual disappearance of the subtler arts of cricket, such as spin bowling, could easily be allayed if a minimum number of overs per day were to be ordained. Fines, in terms of runs to the opposition, could then be extracted from four-pronged pace attack offenders. It all seems so terribly simple to me. But there again, I'm a woman.

What really must be rectified, and with a touch of speed, are the criteria applied in the selection of a touring team. Forget the *Wisdens*, the county averages and the selectors' blue-eyed boys for the moment. Has anyone, for example, ever thought of giving prospective candidates a literacy test? I am absolutely persuaded that there would be far fewer bored cricketers allegedly screwing around (and causing sensations) if only they knew how to get the most out of a book in bed. You think I'm joking? Also, players who do not *want* to be on the tour should be told not to bother coming. It seems so very obvious, doesn't it? And it would save the T.C.C.B. a mint of money in senior official's 'please, please stay!' off-to-the-Caribbean-in-the-winter pleading missions.

A suitably discreet, pre-tour questionnaire (to be treated, of course, in utmost confidence) might look like this:

OFFICIAL T.C.C.B. QUESTIONNAIRE

1. Come off it, now you've got a million in the bank do you *really* want to go on this tour?
2. Come off it, you can tell us, you could never really read, could you?

And everyone, (apart, that is, from Matthew Engel) should be obliged to fill it in.

Much of this diary, it is true, seems to have been devoted to the press. That, I'm afraid, was inevitable. There was so little interesting cricket and so much fascinating press. It may well be, of course, that if cricket tours continue to be inundated with sensation-seeking newshounds, then the traditionally cosy arrangements of yesteryear (when a relative handful of cricket correspondents were accommodated with the players), will have to be altered. John Jackson of the *Daily Mirror* told me, for instance, that during his next assignment for the World Cup in Mexico, the press would be kept completely segregated from the footballers, and official communiqués from team spokesmen would be the only media lifeline to the players. I asked Phil if he thought a similar divorce might be in the offing for England cricket tours.

'I sincerely hope not!' he replied emphatically. 'That would leave the likes of me lumbered with the cricketers!'

Touring can be a beastly business. It is a sequence of constant upheavals only temporarily offset by the occasional euphoria of winning. When the demon of defeatism takes a team by the throat, however, it requires a very special spirit, or a very special character, to tear him off. Neither has been in evidence on this tour.

The game is also suffering from a confused dichotomy: amateur when it should be professional as regards practice, fitness and determination. And dourly professional when it should be amateur, as regards enjoying the odd British High Commissioner's cocktail party without the need for a three line whip to guarantee attendance. Oh, where are you now, dear C.B. Fry?

I am certainly not unhappy to leave that Caribbean maelstrom, and to be back here amid a burgeoning English spring. Not for long however. Tomorrow I return to my interpreters' confraternity for the World Economic Summit in Tokyo — the Heads of State and Government of the World's seven most highly industrialized nations, convened together under one roof — President Reagan of the United States; Mrs Thatcher of the United Kingdom; President Mitterand cum M. Chirac of France; Mr Nakasone of Japan; Mr Craxi of Italy; Chancellor Kohl of the Federal Republic of Germany; and Mr Mulroney of Canada, along with their respective Foreign and Finance Ministers.

Interesting phenomenon, isn't it? I must have located the only group in existence who have even more people gunning for them than the 1986 England touring side to the West Indies!

Test Matches

1st   February 21—23
       Kingston, Jamaica

       England   159, 152
       West Indies 307, 5

       West Indies won by 10 wickets

2nd   March 7—9, 11, 12
       Port-of-Spain, Trinidad

       England   176, 315
       West Indies 399, 95

       West Indies won by 7 wickets

3rd   March 21—23, 25
       Bridgetown, Barbados

       West Indies 418
       England   189, 199

       West Indies won by an innings and 30 runs

4th   April 3—5
       Port-of-Spain, Trinidad

       England   200, 150
       West Indies 312, 39

       West Indies won by 10 wickets

5th   April 11—13, 15, 16
       St John's, Antigua

       West Indies 474, 246
       England   310, 170

       West Indies won by 240 runs

West Indies won series 5—0

One-day Internationals

1st   February 18
      Kingston, Jamaica

      England   145
      West Indies   146

      West Indies won by 6 wickets

2nd   March 4
      Port-of-Spain, Trinidad

      West Indies   229
      England   230

      England won by 5 wickets

3rd   March 19
      Bridgetown, Barbados

      West Indies   249
      England   114

      West Indies won by 135 runs

4th   March 31
      Port-of-Spain, Trinidad

      England   165
      West Indies   166

      West Indies won by 8 wickets

West Indies won series 3—1

Fontana Paperbacks
Non-fiction

Fontana is a leading paperback publisher of non-fiction. Below are some recent titles.

- ☐ McCartney: The Biography *Chet Flippo* £4.50
- ☐ Shirley Temple: American Princess *Anne Edwards* £4.50
- ☐ The Salad Days *Douglas Fairbanks Jr* £4.95
- ☐ Jane Fonda *Michael Freedland* £3.95
- ☐ Oh I Say! *Dan Maskell* £4.50
- ☐ The Thirties and After *Stephen Spender* £2.50
- ☐ If Voting Changed Anything, They'd Abolish It
     Ken Livingstone £3.95
- ☐ The Boys and the Butterflies *James Birdsall* £2.95

You can buy Fontana paperbacks at your local bookshop or newsagent. Or you can order them from Fontana Paperbacks, Cash Sales Department, Box 29, Douglas, Isle of Man. Please send a cheque, postal or money order (not currency) worth the purchase price plus 22p per book for postage (maximum postage required is £3).

NAME (Block letters) _____

ADDRESS _____

_____

_____